S.E.T.

Proceed and Succeed in Your Career

Winning Perspectives for Career Navigation and Success

NATALIE ROWE
Certified Human Resources Professional

To my husband, Seymour Rowe. Without your gentle encouragement and steady support, this book would never have seen the light of day. It is a privilege to partner with you in this journey of life. Thank you infinitely.

I extend my heartfelt gratitude to my family and friends who opened opportunities that fertilized the idea for this book, shared their insights, and offered invaluable comments and encouragement.

CONTENTS

Icons used in the book

Note well

Resource

Activity

4

This book is inspired by a parable told by Jesus Christ of Nazareth

The Parable of the Talents:

"(God's Kingdom) It's also like a man going off on an extended trip. He called his servants together and delegated responsibilities. To one he gave five thousand dollars, to another two thousand, to a third one thousand, depending on their abilities. Then he left. Right off, the first servant went to work and doubled his master's investment. The second did the same. But the man with the single thousand dug a hole and carefully buried his master's money. "After a long absence, the master of those three servants came back and settled up with them. The one given five thousand dollars showed him how he had doubled his investment. His master commended him: 'Good work! You did your job well. From now on be my partner.' "The servant with the two thousand showed how he also had doubled his master's investment. His master commended him: 'Good work! You did your job well. From now on be my partner.' "The servant given one thousand said, 'Master, I know you have high standards and hate careless ways, that you demand the best and make no allowances for error. I was afraid I might disappoint you, so I found a good hiding place and secured your money. Here it is, safe and sound down to the last cent.' "The master was furious. 'That's a terrible way to live! It's criminal to live cautiously like that! If you knew I was after the best, why did you do less than the least? The least you could have done would have been to invest the sum with the bankers, where at least I would have gotten a little interest. "'Take the thousand and give it to the one who risked the most. And get rid of this "play-it-safe" who won't go out on a limb. Throw him out into utter darkness."'[1]

---

[1] Matthew 25:14-30 – The Holy Bible, The Message Version.

6

PREFACE

I was chatting with a friend recently when she commented, "You know, I was wondering about the purpose of being on earth – why are people really here?" Although she is close to retirement, this question lingers. Whether young or mature, the "why" of our existence on earth echoes in the heart for a satisfying answer.

Are you wondering why you are here on earth, what talents you have, and what to do with them? Maybe you have accepted that you are here for a purpose which you are yet to identify. You may be an adolescent facing the decision of which course of study to pursue after high school; or a post-secondary graduate, with a degree and student loan debt, who is still uncertain of the career to pursue. You may be in a job that barely pays the bills or even in a job that pays well. Nevertheless, you feel like part of you is suffocating – some days you look at your tasks and think, "This is not my life; it cannot be."

Maybe you have been satisfyingly employed, and over time, your fire and drive have dwindled, and you are feeling the tug of "something more." Maybe you are on the brink of retirement, or even in retirement, and you are feeling uncertain or even scared of the future. How will you run the home-stretch course of your life? You may be a parent who is pre-occupied with questions about the career of your teen. You may even be uncertain how to best support them to chart the course of their future. If you relate to any of these scenarios, you are not alone. These feelings are more common than you realize.

This book offers winning perspectives for career navigation and success. Ultimately, it's about teaching you where and how to successfully fish for your career. In the process, it will address the three indispensable steps to career navigation and success – Self-awareness, Environment-awareness, and Trained Talents and Personality (S.E.T.).

There are many excellent books available that contain time-tested and proven career advice (visit your local library to start). For that reason, S.E.T. seeks to complement those works and serve as a companion to career advice literature by positioning your mindset to maximize the use of those career tips and strategies. Follow the pages with this goal in mind, as they propose a champion's mentality for facing the inevitable challenges along your career path.

I recommend this book to parents, guidance counsellors, youth leaders and anyone who influences adolescents. The content will equip you to support and guide the decisions of youths to navigate careers that are both successful and authentic to them. In fact, these perspectives will help to nurture the interests of children from their infancy.

I recommend S.E.T. to youths, to focus your thoughts on perspectives that will guide you to invest your efforts and resources into areas that will bring you career satisfaction. To adults and professionals, it is never too late to make that career move that will bring you the fulfillment you have always wanted. S.E.T. proposes a mindset that will help you break free from mental limitations that can leave you feeling stuck and discouraged by the challenges of your environment.

True work is life-long. So if you are retired or close to retirement, the S.E.T. perspectives will help you to invest your time on your terms and to your satisfaction, whether in your family, the community, or with an organization. Whatever your stage on the journey of life, I invite you to explore some universal perspectives that I believe will focus your thoughts on truths that will inspire confidence in your career decisions.

Introduction

The Purpose of Your Career

As I pen these pages, I am on the cusp of repositioning in my career. I have been blessed with successful and satisfying assignments. Now I have chosen to respond to the exciting and daunting call of "something more." This book is as much a product as it is a journey for me as I seek to, once again, walk out the very advice written on these pages. I know the plethora of emotions that show up at decision time for career – ranging from the excitement of possibilities to the fear of uncertainties.

I have had many career conversations with people and have been a first-hand witness to feelings of unbridled optimism to those of doubt, discouragement, and even despair. Such can be the rollercoaster ride of emotions surrounding career decisions. However, I am confident that these highs and lows can be successfully navigated if you adopt and cultivate a proactive mindset that places you in the driver's seat of your career decisions. This will require you to embrace perspectives that both guard your mind from discouragement and guide your decisions towards fulfilling your purpose.

Your understanding of the purpose of work places you in a position to add value that goes beyond a job description. It provides a context that inspires and energizes you for the tasks at hand. Three men were seen doing the same task and were asked to explain their work. This first man replied that he was laying bricks, the second man said he was building a wall, and the third man explained that he was building a library.

As far as purpose is concerned, you may likely agree that the third person gave the most enlightened response. This insight also positioned the third worker to add the greatest value to the project. Perhaps, while laying the bricks, his understanding of the purpose of his work may prompt him to recommend the use of glass panels at certain sections of the library walls for a more pleasant user-experience. When you understand that you are a part of something that is bigger than the task at hand, you will likely feel more empowered, and be more productive and fulfilled.

We each likely embrace a narrative that explains the reality of our existence. Several theories seek to explain the *how* of our human existence but they fall short of explaining the *why*. I find that the Biblical narrative answers both the *how* and *why* of our existence. It is a narrative that provides the context for work, which is meant to positively impact the person and their environment, and connects human beings to a mandate that is way greater than any we could ever have conceived for ourselves.

So why are you here on planet earth? I gleaned an insight from the *Parable of the Talents* referenced at the beginning of this book. You are here on earth to partner with God – note that partnering with God was the reward to the servants who took the risk of increasing their seed money. This begs the question, "Partner to do what?" The Lord's Prayer gives another insight – *"Thy kingdom come. Thy will be done on earth, as it is in heaven. [2]* Our assignment on planet earth is to partner with God in the pursuit of making earth like heaven. This quest requires the participation of every human being. By extension, this means that each person has an assignment, and in effect, each person has a career to pursue.

Whatever your career, the ultimate purpose is to make your little corner of earth like heaven. If you are a teacher, your career supports the eradication of ignorance, since there is perfect knowledge in heaven; if a chef, to make food tasty, like it is in heaven; if an entertainer, to bring pleasure, since heaven is a place of unending pleasures; if a lawyer, to promote justice, since heaven is a place of perfect justice; if a sanitation worker, to promote cleanliness, as it is in heaven, and so on. Whether you are aware or not, every good pursuit is about making earth function like heaven.

---

[2] Matthew 6:10 KJV.

The Seed and Soil of Your Career

"My job is somehow not secure at all." "We want a chance to work, we want to prove ourselves." "*My academic training did not prepare me for my employment."* These are some of the views expressed by youths on the issue of employment, as presented in *The United Nations World Youth Report 2011*. The opinions capture the heartfelt desire of youths to contribute to their environment and be compensated in ways that create stability and satisfaction.

With closer examination, I could not help but note the foundational beliefs of these sentiments, which I speculate to be, *"my job should give me a sense of security"; "someone should ensure that there are adequate jobs available;"* and "*someone should have ensured that my studies prepared me for my job.*" But what if you chose to have a perspective towards your employment that focused more on your abilities rather than on the outlet (job) for those abilities? What if you saw your income security as rooted in your abilities rather than in a job? What if you placed the onus on yourself to make your work happen rather than on someone else to make it happen for you? What if you made it your responsibility to ensure that your studies prepared you for your work? What if you saw your work as life-long instead of for a period of time? Such perspectives would open new windows of possibilities that could bring hope and security in your future.

Notwithstanding, there are situations of frustration and uncertainty at each step of the career continuum – from career exploration to career advancement, and even into retirement. Anxieties persist, sometimes to the point of depression, in the presence of excellent career advice and tools to guide each stage.

If the tips to realizing a successful career are seeds, then the perspective or mentality that you hold towards your career is the soil. Every farmer knows that the combination of high quality seed and nutrient-rich soil is necessary for a bumper harvest. In my experience, I have learned that an awareness of the mentality that you carry towards your career determines whether good career advice produces the harvest of satisfaction that you seek. It is easy to neglect the worldview that you carry towards your career because it is not obvious.

It is much like the foundation of a house that is usually only examined when there is a problem or an imminent transaction. If you are showing a friend your new house, you will tend to focus on the layout, fixtures, and features that are obvious to the eye. You do this because you assume that the foundation is sound. However, if the foundation *is* the problem, then its condition will compromise the structure of the home, notwithstanding the granite countertops, marble floors, and exquisite crown moldings.

Perspectives determine focus, and focus determines what is seen, and what is not seen. Could it be that the seed of good career advice is being choked by perspectives that deprive them of nutrients? For this reason, the motivation for this book is to address the mentality you hold concerning your career. Its intent is to increase awareness of the foundational beliefs and perspectives that nurture a successful career in order to focus your thoughts on that which will keep you supple, relevant, resilient, and creating value in an increasingly dynamic world.

So Simple, It's Easy to Miss

Some time ago, not long after I had given birth, and as is often the case with mothers after delivery, I was in a hurry to lose the "baby fat." I was at home watching a documentary special on television featuring a famous American chef. His cuisine was so highly sought after that people stood in line for hours to patronize his restaurant. He was obviously overweight. At a point in the interview, he was asked to share the secret to his recent substantial weight-loss. My ears perked up as I thought that I could certainly use his effective weight-loss strategy to lose a mere 20 pounds. As usual, the answer would come only after the commercial break! I used this unwelcomed delay to prepare to take good notes. Finally, the feature continued. When posed the question about his weight-loss, he nonchalantly responded, "Oh, I just started eating less." In my mind I nudged him on... and...? I don't recall him adding much more to the point. His manner appeared "no-brainer-like" and he seemed ready for the next question. I was most disappointed because I was listening for the spectacular – something complicated and perhaps more challenging. After recovering from the "let-down" and reflecting on what he said, it made perfect sense. All things being equal, if you eat less, you will lose weight!

This occurrence has always reminded me of the power of practicing simple truths. If we are honest with ourselves, we will admit that we all have information that has not been beneficial to us because we have failed to *act* on the knowledge. I read somewhere that each person has several ideas in their lifetime that could make them millionaires, except they do not act.

Success in any area is found in acting on a good idea – it's no different with your career. Whether you are a parent seeking ideas on how to best support your child in their career search, a student exploring career options, a worker or professional at the crossroads of a career change, or a retiree, as you read through these pages on career perspectives, my desire for you is to act on simple truths. Knowing is a good start, but acting on the right information is what gets you the results you desire. Promise yourself to act in your best interest. Your life is not a dress rehearsal. You are living out the feature presentation and time passes quickly.

Your Career Matters

There Are Needs to Meet

"You aren't alive if you aren't in need." – Henry Cloud

Your career matters because there are needs to be met at the level of the individual and of society. No one can effectively meet all their physical, emotional, and spiritual needs on their own. The saying that no man is an island holds true, even more so in a globalized and internationally connected world. Simply put, **we pay others to meet our needs when those needs are brought to the marketplace**. For example, we pay for a hand-held device to meet our communication and information needs. We pay a grocer to deliver food to our table. We pay daycare providers to care for our children as we work, while our employers pay us to meet the needs of their clients. It is a cycle. When others pay us to meet their needs, we pay others to meet our own needs.

Needs never go into recession. As long as people are alive, needs exist. Consider that whether the stock market goes up or down, you still need to eat, wear, and sleep. The thing that will likely change with your income is the way in which you eat, wear, and sleep. Therefore, the part that changes with economic movements is *how* people meet their needs. For example, people living in the 4th century needed to communicate with each other, and that need remains today. However, the ways in which people communicate in these two eras are vastly different. **Careers, therefore, arise from the existence of needs and the human inter-dependence required to meet those needs.** These two factors ensure that everyone can be employed in the business of meeting needs.

The root meaning of the word career comes from the Latin *carrus*, which means "chariot"; Also, *cararia,* which means "carriage or road, track for wheeled vehicles." The word also means "a running" or "a course, of say, the sun across the sky." [3] These definitions suggest that a career is both a vessel and a path that enables passage from one place to the next. Career, therefore, refers to the body of work[4] that you undertake to make your contribution to life. This work will both carry you through life by satisfying your needs, and creating a path for you to advance.

🛈 In essence, **your career is both your transporter and navigator to shuttle you through the course of life.**

In common use, when you hear reference to a career, it usually refers to work undertaken in a particular field[5] over a significant period of the person's life that also offers the opportunity for progress. That said, a career may span more than one field, as in a teacher turned entertainer then politician. A career may also involve different jobs[6] in related fields, such as a paramedic becoming a nurse and then family doctor. It may involve different jobs with increasing responsibilities in the same field, such as a book-keeper working their way to becoming partner in a firm, or a farm-help becoming the manager/owner of the farm. A career may also involve keeping the same type of job from graduation to retirement, as in an electrician or mechanic.

Whether one chooses to focus their career in one field, or chooses to move their career across fields; the common thread running through all of the preceding examples of career is that work is done to meet needs in a chosen field(s), at a chosen level(s), and over a period of time. There is also the expectation that a career brings satisfaction and opportunities to develop personally and professionally.

🛈 **Whatever your chosen field, your career matters because each career is about meeting needs**. The inter-relationship of needs implies that if you forfeit the pursuit of your career, you are, in effect, forfeiting your responsibility to meet your own needs and those of others. Think of persons who dared to step out and pursue their passion. In addition to creating a product or service that benefits others, they may have also created jobs and an outlet for the talents of others. Now consider if they had done nothing to pursue their passion, how different would

---

[3] Online Etymology Dictionary. www.etymonline.com (accessed September 12, 2016).
[4] Any task that employs the mind and/or body.
[5] The word "field" may be broadly or narrowly defined. Synonyms include subject or discipline.
[6] Defined set of tasks.

life be for you? The next time you enjoy the benefits of a product or service or see an enterprise, take a moment to be grateful for the person(s) who dared to face the risks of pursuing their career.

The impact of neglecting to pursue a career fuels a vicious cycle where, being unable to pay others to meet your own needs (and since your needs never go away), you open the door to lack, dependency, and even dishonest means. However, you have the power to stop this vicious cycle of lack by creating a virtuous cycle of meeting needs. This will require you to give the necessary attention to the decisions that are in favour of realizing your career.

You Can Meet Needs

"How wonderful it is that nobody need wait a single moment before starting to improve the world." – Anne Frank

Your career matters because you have the ability to meet needs. Each person was born with their own portion. Another way to see it is that **we all came into this world with start-up capital.** To demonstrate this point with an extreme example, my friend was in a hospice towards the end of her life. I was in my third trimester of pregnancy and I often visited her after work. As I walked down the corridors of the institution towards her room, I noted patients of all ages and in varying degrees of incapacitation. They mostly lay on their backs and required help to even change positions in their beds. No matter how tired I was after a demanding day at the office, I always felt invigorated when leaving the hospice. Somehow the condition of the patients was a reminder to be thankful that I could move my own body and that even the feeling of tiredness was a result of the capacity that I had to work. In their own way, perhaps unknown to them, the patients were meeting my need for inspiration, a change of perspective, and a reminder to be grateful in all things.

It is important to realize that you have an inherent ability to meet needs. Depending on the circumstances, some abilities express themselves in passive ways, as in the example I just described, while at other times, they express themselves in active ways, as in the work of, say, a caregiver. Whether the abilities you have to meet needs are expressed passively or actively, it is important to be aware that you have them. **Everyone can do something to make a positive difference to others**.

People don't always get paid when they meet a need because not all abilities are brought to the marketplace. However, when properly developed and packaged, all abilities have the potential to receive payment when they meet a need. **No one can take your abilities from you, but you have the choice to recognize and develop them, or devalue and ignore them**. I will go into detail about this point later in the book.

For now, the mere fact that you have inborn abilities presents you with the question of what to do with them. The answer is yours to seek and will point you to your career.

You Will Hold Yourself Accountable

So then every one of us shall give account of himself to God.
– Romans 14:12 KJV.

Your career matters because you will hold yourself accountable for the decisions you make concerning it. Human beings habitually assess their decisions. The emotion of regret testifies to the accountability that we naturally require of ourselves for the choices we make. The feeling is experienced after we perform a stock-taking exercise on our decisions. It is the feeling that something went wrong, that another course should have been taken. We somehow know that we should have chosen differently.

In a study by Roese and Summerville[7] on "What We Regret Most … and Why," over three thousand participants rated education and career as their top two regrets, followed by romance, parenting, self-improvement, and leisure. The study concluded that opportunity breeds regret and that the feelings of dissatisfaction and disappointment were strongest where the chances to capitalize were the greatest.

Roese indicates that when the emotion of regret is used in a productive way, it has significant value. His studies of younger people showed that regret was rated relatively favourable, primarily because of its informational value in motivating corrective action. Regret was rated most favourable on a list of negative

---

[7] Roese, Neal and Summerville, Amy. "What We Regret Most… and Why." http://journals.sagepub.com/doi pdf/10.1177/0146167205274693 (accessed October 16, 2016).

emotions because it helped people to make sense of the world and avoid future negative behaviours, sparked insight, achieved social harmony, and improved approaches to opportunities. When used unproductively, regret may lead to excessive rumination, depression, or even suicide, as in the reported case in *The Harvard Newsletter* of a man in Liverpool who committed suicide after forgetting to renew his lottery ticket, which he habitually bought, on the day that his numbers were drawn.

Rick Breden, president of psychological testing and behaviour analytics firm, Essentials, says, **"Most of the time regrets center around what you didn't do, not what you did. You regret not trying something."** [8] It is not surprising that education and career are the top two regrets, as the opportunities to learn and meet needs have never been greater. The Internet has revolutionized the way people connect, and made access to learning easier and cheaper by reducing the costs posed by physical limitations. For the same reasons, it has also facilitated the creation of new careers and businesses through flexible work arrangements and simplified access to people and resources.

The research studies on regret suggest that the greater the opportunity to have changed an outcome, the stronger the emotion of regret. They also suggest that over short periods of time, regret is usually expressed for actions taken and mistakes made. However, over long periods of time, regret is expressed for actions *not* taken.

Give yourself the opportunity to stock-take your life savoring the sweet wine of career satisfaction instead of the bitter gall of regret. Make choices so that you will have answers to the inevitable "what if" questions – what if I had done *that* or what if I had chosen *this*? When you act on the opportunities of today, you will know the answers to these questions because you had in fact done *that* and chosen *this*.

It is the privilege of human beings to choose and to live with the outcome of their choices. The decisions that you make today concerning your career will determine the outcome that you will entertain tomorrow. This is one of my reasons for proactively seeking a new career assignment. Persons looking on may question my decision, granted the privileges of my

---

[8] Source: Market Watch Personal Finance. http://www.themoneystreet.com/one-of-the-biggest-life-regrets-for-older-americans-is/ (accessed October 16, 2016).

current assignment. However, I choose to give myself permission to discover what is behind that inner nudge forward. I have heard it said that *what you are looking for is also looking for you.* I must uncover those other, perhaps greater, needs that are seeking me. Whatever the outcome, I know that stepping-out has favourably positioned me to confidently reflect on my life having the answers to my "what-if" career questions.

The remainder of this book assumes that you have made the decision to seek the answer to the question of what to do with your inborn talents – even if you are not yet aware of them. If you are still uncertain of your position concerning your career journey, read on. A decision can be made at any point.

Your Mindset Matters

(!) The lens through which things are viewed determines what is seen (and what is not seen), and thereby dictates the response. You may have heard the story of the two shoe salesmen whose company sent them to a remote village to explore new markets for shoes. Upon arrival, one salesman sent a message home saying, "No one here wears shoes; I have no choice but to return home soon." The other salesman sent this message: "No one here wears shoes; send inventory!" Interestingly, both salesmen faced the same reality of a shoeless market. One salesman assumed that he could do nothing to change this situation. While, the other salesman saw an opportunity to change the market by simultaneously meeting the need for shoes and making money for his company. No doubt, the career trajectory of these salesmen went in opposite directions – all determined by their mindset.

(!) Often, perspective is the deciding factor between success and failure, and average and extraordinary. It is for this reason that this section of the book is dedicated to examining and proposing winning perspectives towards your career. These universal perspectives are crucial to master at every stage on your career journey.

The Value in Obstacles

"Price is what you pay. Value is what you get." – Warren Buffett

The word "obstacle" means to "stand before, stand opposite to, block, hinder"[9]. Based on this definition, the thought of an obstacle tends to elicit the response of a sigh, perhaps an eye-roll, feeling of resentment, frustration, or even anger. However, there are always alternative ways of looking at a thing. In fact, **obstacles are more than hindrances. They are also life's way of confirming that you have the qualification to do the job or the required level of responsibility to manage that which you seek to possess.**

This can be demonstrated by the example of a person being allowed to fly a passenger jet on the sole basis of a passion to do so, without having to face the process of testing and certification. It is easy to see that much injury and disaster would follow such a practice. To prevent this occurrence, pre-requisites are put in place to ensure that anyone flying a passenger jet has been proven qualified to do so. For this reason, the pre-requisites or obstacles are an integral means of protecting society against incompetence and the resulting injury.

You may consider the certification required to pursue a particular career to be more of a pre-requisite than an obstacle. However, failure to achieve the certification in question will stand in the way of you pursuing the career. Usually, a pre-requisite becomes an obstacle in your mind when you find it challenging to meet. Given that we each face differing circumstances and have varying abilities, what may be viewed as a pre-requisite for one person may be seen as an obstacle to another person. This means that a pre-requisite and an obstacle are, *in essence*, one and the same (much like ice and water) because either one can hinder desired progress when their conditions are not satisfied.

How you view the pre-requisites for working in a chosen career, will likely influence how you respond to the prospect of working in that field. To explain, if you view the certification required to be an electrician as a pre-requisite, you may be more willing to research the steps involved, contact the institutions that offer the certification, and get information on the associated costs and time required to achieve the certification. On the other hand, if you view the same pre-requisite as an obstacle, then an inherent negative view of obstacles will likely sap your desire to seek the information that could help you certify as an electrician.

---

[9] Online Etymology Dictionary. www.etymonline.com (accessed October 12, 2016).

(!) **In order to cultivate a winning mindset towards your career, choose to view obstacles to your career (or pre-requisites) in a positive light[10] by replacing negative thoughts towards obstacles with positive ones**. For example, instead of seeing the pre-requisite for your chosen career as a hindrance to you entering or advancing in that profession, you could see the recommended certification as protection from potential loss.

Just as obstacles are necessary to protect society, they are also necessary to protect you from the consequences of under-preparation for the job. Living in a country that has two official languages, it is easy to complain about the hindrance of bilingualism to career advancement when you are unilingual. However, instead of viewing the bilingualism requirement for certain jobs as an obstacle, one could embrace the opportunity to learn another language as a privilege. All other things being equal, a more positive mindset will prove advantageous to developing proficiency in another language. Bilingualism will increase your competence to meet the needs of your environment and open opportunities to more jobs.

Another perspective to hold in the process of cultivating a positive view of obstacles is to recognize that obstacles are non-discriminatory in that everyone desiring a particular thing has to face them. Then, **through a process of self-selection, each person decides whether to possess their desired career by their decision to invest the effort required to overcome the obstacles that are in their way**. All things being equal, anyone can become a pilot or an accountant if they are willing to do the work involved to meet the respective pre-requisites. Again, people have varying abilities and face varying limitations, so the invested effort will differ from one person to another.

A friend shared how the effects of dyslexia[11] required him to study three times longer than the average student. Throughout his studies to graduate school, he was not aware of the learning disability. All he knew was that he had to read and re-read his notes several times before he could grasp the concepts (he was later diagnosed with the condition while in his professional career). However, he decided that if studying for significantly longer hours

---

[10] The discussion that follows assumes that pre-requisites and obstacles are one and the same, and are applied fairly.
[11] Disorder that involve difficulty in learning to read or interpret words, letters, and other symbols, but that do not affect general intelligence.

than his peers was what it took for him to graduate, then so be it. He applied himself to learning, which reduced the time he had to fraternize with his friends.

His decision to dedicate most of his time to studying resulted in him completing his graduate degree with honours. He also commented that in certain ways, he is happy that he was ignorant of the learning condition, as he may have used it as an excuse to avoid doing his best. The point to note is that a pre-requisite to a career is the same for everyone. That said, given our individual capacities, expect the effort invested to achieve what is required to vary. However, **if you are willing to invest the required effort to achieve the pre-requisite or overcome the obstacle to your career, it places you on common footing with everyone who possesses that pre-requisite.**

An equally important view that can contribute to nurturing a positive mindset towards obstacles is to acknowledge the profound truth that **everything (including your career) has a price**. It is therefore worthwhile to appreciate the indispensable role that pricing plays in society. Whatever the obstacles to your career – finances, certification, time, access – they represent the price of operating in the career that you seek.

To highlight the importance of pricing, imagine a scenario in which each shopper in a store decides the price of their purchases. Perhaps some shoppers would pay nothing, most would pay something, and others might even pay more than fair market value. Each person would likely pay a price convenient to them at that moment. While that would work well for the shopper, what impact would that have on the seller?

A product that required the highest quality materials, the use of specialized knowledge, hours of intricate and painstaking labour to produce, and then had to be transported across oceans and highways to the store, could have shoppers pay little or nothing to walk away with it in their shopping bags. How is that fair to all the labour that went into making the item? Shouldn't the producers be fairly compensated for their efforts, risks and investment?

Such a cycle would be unsustainable. Before long, production of that item would cease for lack of fair compensation to the producers. There is also the impact of this scenario on the buyer. In their mind, the low price that they paid signaled a low product value. As a result, their careless misuse of the item did not permit them to discover the full benefit of the product.

It is a natural human tendency to treat things based on the price paid – whether in effort, sacrifice, or money. In this example, the low price paid for the item resulted in two injustices – an unfair compensation to the producers and the misuse of the item by the buyer. **For these reasons, pricing is necessary to protect the sustainability of the process, as well as to promote fairness to both the producer and buyer.** In the same way, it is necessary to overcome obstacles in the pursuit of a career, as they play a similar role in protecting the practice and sustainability of your desired career and promoting fair compensation. **Obstacles, in effect, reflect the value of functioning in a career.**

In general, pricing is required to manage the human tendency of "easy come, easy go." This reality plays out daily when parents express frustration at their children for the abuse of things and opportunities that are bought by hard-earned money. Politicians and administrators face the challenge of minimizing the abuse of tax-payer funded programs and facilities. For the same reason, insurance companies charge a deductible for every claim made to discourage the human tendency to treat things carelessly when there is no cost to the claimant – referred to as moral hazard. Businesses also recognize this human tendency to attach worth to price. I once read that fragrances provide one of the largest profit margins to retail stores because buyers believe that the more expensive the fragrance, the better the quality. For that reason, the fragrance section is always placed at the main entrance of stores.

Even our natural laws play out the scenario of "everything has a price." Newton's third law of motion states that, "For every action, there is an equal (in size) and opposite (in direction) reaction force." It describes that forces result from interactions that always come in pairs – known as "action-reaction force pairs." If you throw a ball forward, the "price" of the thrust is that the ball will push back at you with equal force (try doing it on roller blades to experience the push-back force).

So it is in life. You will experience push-back on every effort you make to move forward. Do not be deterred by this. Rather, respect the value in the obstacle. **If there is no resistance, then there is no value to be gained. Resistance is a statement of worth**. The more valuable a thing, the more obstacles you must overcome to possess it, just as the higher the value of a thing, the greater the surrounding security detail. This relationship recognizes the worth of everything, and in so doing, establishes balance that is necessary for sustainability.

Given the multifaceted role that obstacles (pre-requisites) play in the world of careers by confirming qualification, protecting against injury, promoting fairness and sustainability, and signaling value, it follows that obstacles are to be viewed with respect and appreciation (instead of annoyance), knowing that they signal the worth of that which you desire. In other words, think of an obstacle as a chest that contains valuable treasure. In the same vein, be encouraged in knowing that **the obstacles that you face in choosing, qualifying, and advancing in your career are, in effect, signals of the importance and worth of functioning in your career**.

Worth Transfer

"There are no short cuts to any place worth going." – Helen Keller

Few things in life come "ready to use." Most things must undergo processing in order for their benefits to be enjoyed. Given that obstacles are a signal of worth, it is important to know how to access that worth. **When you commit yourself to pushing against an obstacle in the correct way, you are actually igniting the process of "worth transfer,"** as demonstrated by the examples that follow:

Your effort to become a doctor means that you have to overcome the obstacle of a medical certification. As you apply your mind, body, time, and finances to obtaining the degree, you are transferring the worth of that certification to yourself. Upon graduation, you own that worth because you paid the price.

When you seek to get your body in shape, you apply yourself to activities of physical resistance. As you train, you are transferring the worth contained in the weights and cardio-vascular activities into your very body. With persistence, a fit physique will be yours – the price paid was pressure to your body.

When you seek to develop mental and moral strength, you need to push back against deception and immoral choices. In so doing, your mentality and morality will be strengthened by the pressures of deceit. As you push back against those temptations, your choices implicitly strengthen your character. It is for these reasons that people who have paid the price to overcome obstacles are admired, seen as great, and even envied.

When you pay the price for an item, you can walk confidently with it out of the store. Even if the anti-theft buzzer goes off, without hesitation, you may show your receipt when questioned because the item is legitimately yours. If you had shop-lifted, you would likely drop the goods and run. This is often what happens to people who do not pay the price to advance in influence and wealth. Soon the pressures of demands and expectations overwhelm their under-prepared mental and other capacities, and may lead to self-destructive tendencies.

(!) **To bypass the legitimate process of worth transfer is also to bypass the opportunity to develop the mental, professional, and psychological acumen required to support the weight of that which has been acquired**. The following excerpt shows the value that is contained in appropriately pushing past obstacles, *"The Cecropia moth emerges from its cocoon only after a long, exhausting struggle to free itself. A young boy, wishing to help the moth, carefully slit the exterior of the cocoon. Soon it came out, but its wings were shriveled and couldn't function. What the boy did not realize was that the moth's struggle to liberate itself from the cocoon was essential to develop its wings – and its ability to fly.[12] "*

It is beneficial to push against obstacles in the correct way in order to transfer all the worth that they contain. For example, training to become a doctor takes years of commitment to study, which will likely mean sleepless nights and other sacrifices. This very process presents the opportunity to develop the characteristics of perseverance and discipline to achieve medical competence – the very qualities needed to be a good physician. Should a

---

[12] Dayton, Howard. Navigating Your Finances God's Way, Canadian Edition. Orlando, Florida: Compass – Finances God's Way, 2015.

student cheat their way through medical school, they are also cheating themselves of the requisite skills and character that build competence. Incompetence would soon lead to malpractice or even loss of medical license. When you pay the price of overcoming the obstacles to develop your talents and pursue your career, you can be confident in your work. **The strength gained in the process of acquiring a thing is the same strength needed to carry that thing**. It is well advised that you submit yourself correctly to the process of worth transfer.

The extent of your desire for your career will determine your commitment to the process of worth transfer. What does your career mean to you, and how much effort and resources are you willing to invest into making it happen? I read the following excerpt from the Online Etymology Dictionary on the meaning of the word, "obstacle." It says, *"The lover thinks more often of reaching his mistress than the husband of guarding his wife; the prisoner thinks more often of escaping than the gaoler of shutting his door; and so, whatever the obstacles may be, the lover and the prisoner ought to succeed."*[13] The excerpt highlights the role of desire in overcoming obstacles. Although it appears wayward that it recommends that the immoral intentions succeed, the basis of that recommendation should not be overlooked – that is, **success is blind and rules in favour of effort rather than entitlement**. In other words, it is fair for success to come to the one who not only wants it more, but who is also willing to invest the effort to realize it. There is indeed something special and rewarding about investing the required effort to pursue your vocation. **Career success is not an entitlement; it is a reward to those who diligently seek it.**

To summarize, an obstacle is value waiting to be seized. **All things, including obstacles, have worth. When you choose to do the work to make that worth yours, the accomplishment will in turn unveil the worth that you always had in you.** Your understanding of the value in obstacles and the process of worth transfer positions you to confidently invest your efforts into your career choices.

---

[13] www.etymonline.com. Stendhal, "Charterhouse of Parma.".

Trying Uncovers Help

He who observes the wind will not sow, and he who regards the clouds will not reap. Ecclesiastes 11:4 NKJV.

An equally important perspective to build your confidence as you pursue your career, is knowing that help is guaranteed along the way. Often, people do not pursue the deep desires of their heart because they cannot see how they will be able to accomplish the goal. They know that they will need help, but they are uncertain of the source. **Whether with your career or any other venture, the "hidden" treasure of help is available to everyone. However, help most often reveals itself to those who are willing to step out and try, despite the obstacles**.

When we bought our first home, my husband and I pursued many do-it-yourself projects in order to save money. In one instance, we decided to lay patio stones. We did not own a wheelbarrow, so my husband improvised and tied a string to a box to remove the sod in order to prepare the foundation for the stones. Soon after, our neighbour stopped by our house with a timely loan. He said that he and his wife saw us working and thought that we could really use a wheelbarrow to help us along. We gladly accepted the offer and remain grateful for their kind gesture.

This simple example underscores the point that trying uncovers help. Not all help needed to achieve a goal will show up at the start of a project or venture, but once you are able[14] to begin – as opposed to comfortable to begin – go ahead. My husband and I could have chosen to delay or abandon the project because we did not have all the tools. The result would be that our neighbour would never have been alerted to the fact that we had a need that they could meet, nor would we have our desired patio stones. It was our commitment to doing the home improvement project with what we had that uncovered the help we needed.

The effort of "trying" is like a shovel that unearths the hidden treasure of "help," and when it shows up, it is like a miracle that does wonders to change a situation. You may have heard the story of two mice that fell into a bucket of cream. The first mouse quickly gave up and drowned in

---

[14] You have a workable plan.

the cream. The second mouse wouldn't quit fighting to get air. It struggled so hard that eventually it churned the cream into butter and crawled out. This is another example of the power of "trying." I am certain that both mice wanted to live but one mouse chose to face death by waiting for it, while the other mouse chose to face death by fighting for life.

The efforts of the mouse created a miracle that it did not expect. Every struggle to live was impacting the cream and unwittingly changing it into a substance more favourable to its survival – talk about worth transfer. By pushing back at the cream that threatened its life, the mouse changed the consistency of the cream into something from which it was able to crawl.

Maybe when the mouse shared its ordeal with other mice, some commented that it was lucky. Have you ever worked hard to achieve something – a happy marriage, a successful career, a prosperous business, a healthy lifestyle? You just refused to quit, even though all hope seemed lost – then people look on and declare that you are lucky. How irritating is that! Well, let me tell you what luck is. It is "Labour Under Correct Knowledge" – emphasis on "labour" and on "correct." My high school teacher shared this with us to underscore the point that working diligently comes before success.

(!) **Luck is generated**. I once read an article on the results of a study on luck. It studied the behaviour of people who reported winning more prizes than the average person in the population. The article concluded that these "lucky people" in fact generated their own luck because they entered more prize-draws than the average person in the population. Their luck was simply a result of them increasing their probability to win – the more draws they entered, the more chances they gave themselves to win; hence, the more they actually won. The Roman Philosopher, Seneca, said it best – "Luck is what happens when preparation meets opportunity."

Are you willing to move your life forward? It will take effort and require you to sacrifice your comfort zone, but that is the price of (!) progress. **Every effort you make to improve yourself and advance your career will change your environment and cause it to become more favourable to you**. That is why people with higher educational certifications usually earn more. Their pursuit of learning caused their environment to become more favourable to them.

Upgrading your skills, gaining experience and expertise, and pursuing that certification are efforts that will cause your environment to compensate you more for your ability to meet needs. It all starts with stepping out to try – being willing to do the work to transfer the worth of the obstacle to you.

A friend shared how she had always wanted to be a veterinarian. After college, she only had money to finance one year of the five-year veterinary program that was only offered abroad. She decided to pursue the program anyway in the hopes that something would work in her favour. She worked so hard during that year that she won a full scholarship to complete the program. Simultaneously, the government of her country began to subsidize the same course of study. Between the two new sources of income, she had enough money to cover her living expenses and to send home to help her single mother.

If she had chosen to stay in the place where there was no chance of her ever becoming a veterinarian, and avoid the risk of starting a program that she had no guarantee of finishing, she might never have discovered that the help of a scholarship and funding support were awaiting her. Help indeed reveals itself to those who are willing to face the risk of trying. My friend's efforts were much like a down payment on her future. By stepping out to face the risks, she showed that she was committed to the process.

Have you noticed that you take more pleasure in helping people who are willing to try, rather than those who refuse to go out on a limb in their best interest? People who are willing to help themselves tend to put your help to good use and in no time will wean themselves of your support. On the other hand, those who prefer that you face all the risks so that they can remain in their comfort zone are more likely to squander your help at the first sign of the next challenge. They will also likely need your help longer, and if you permit it[15], become a lifetime dependent.

The process of trying will build your confidence. I know

---

[15] Do not permit it.

of persons returning to school in their senior years, facing the fear of learning how to use the computer to do their assignments. But with persistence, they get help along the way to succeed. If you lack confidence, **nothing builds confidence more than achieving something you thought was difficult**. When it comes to your career, do not hesitate to proceed knowing that obstacles are yours to overcome, and your efforts will uncover the help (in waiting) that you will need to achieve your goals. Trying also means leaving your place of familiarity, so it's important to have a positive perspective on leaving your comfort zone.

The Paradox of the Comfort Zone

"A ship is safe in the harbour, but that's not what ships are for."
– William G.T. Shedd

Advancing in your career will require you to leave your comfort zone, to step out into the unfamiliar, and face uncomfortable situations. It will require that you develop new skills and use your talents in new ways. According to the Cambridge Dictionary, the comfort zone is "a situation in which you feel comfortable and in which your ability and determination are not being tested." Brené Brown, a research professor at the University of Houston Graduate College of Social Work and author of "The Gifts of Imperfection" (Hazelden, 2010), has another definition of comfort zone: "Where our uncertainty, scarcity and vulnerability are minimized — where we believe we'll have access to enough love, food, talent, time, admiration. Where we feel we have some control."[16] A. White states,[17] The comfort zone is a behavioural state within which a person operates in an anxiety-neutral condition, using a limited set of behaviours to deliver a steady level of performance, usually without a sense of risk. These definitions all point to the comfort zone as a place of evenness.

Interestingly, the comfort zone does not always imply an objective state of comfort – it varies from one person to another. Given the ability of human beings to adapt, people can become "comfortable" in disadvantageous circumstances, such as those of control, poverty, sickness, and abuse. I have heard of prisoners who deliberately re-offend with the intention of extending

---

[16] Tugend, Alina. Tiptoeing Out of One's Comfort Zone (and of Course, Back In). New York Times, http://www.nytimes.com/2011/02/12/your-money/12shortcuts.html (accessed October 17, 2016).
[17] White, Alasdair. From Comfort Zone to Performance Management. White and MacLean Publishing, 2008.

their prison terms. Why? Having become comfortable with the predictable lifestyle of incarceration, they are overwhelmed by the prospect of being free to take control of their own lives. There is also the wife who threatened her husband with divorce for having the audacity to suggest that they get off welfare, move out of subsidized housing, and buy their own home. These examples attest to the subjective nature of the comfort zone.

(!) **The comfort zone is a decision for the status quo** – for better or for worse. It is where a person has no impetus for change, or where their desire for change is not strong enough to translate into action that brings change. I have listened to people who express a desire to change their job due to one discomfort or another. However, they often either do not have an exit strategy or, if they do, are not mobilizing it. What usually becomes clear is that the discomforts of the current job have not yet outweighed the advantages of remaining in that position. Action to leave usually only occurs when the reverse becomes true. Suffice it to say that if you want to move forward, then you have to be prepared to do something different, and that decision will likely take you out of your comfort zone.

(!) **The comfort zone is a necessary state. It plays the role of home – a place to relax, refresh, retool, and regenerate**. But to do most things in life, we daily leave our home base: e.g., to buy groceries, go to school, work, travel, and achieve other goals. Most people would agree that leaving home is indispensable to functioning in life. In the same vein, leaving your comfort zone is indispensable to functioning in your career.

It is highly advantageous to nurture a mindset that is willing to try new things despite fears, doubts, and uncertainties. A friend shared her anxiety at the thought of going back to school after being away from the classroom for over two decades. As a single parent on a customer service representative salary, she was clueless as to how she could pursue and pay for an MBA program. Notwithstanding, she could not shake the feeling that she should go ahead. As she stepped out of her comfort zone, financial assistance came in ways she could never have imagined. Now a graduate, she marvels at how she was able to work a 12-hour per day job, parent, and complete her assignments to excel in the program.

The comfort zone also plays the role of thermostat in your life. It is often unease that signals that something is off balance, whether physically, mentally, or emotionally. If you are faced with a situation that you find uncomfortable, listen to the signals that your discomfort is communicating. Is it that you need more information or that you are feeling threatened? Identifying the reasons for your discomfort can help you to address the need and return to a place of comfort.

In fact, it **is your very desire for the comfort zone that will motivate you to regain a new sense of ease and control**. As such, the comfort zone should not be despised, as it performs an essential cautionary and balancing role in your life.

While the comfort zone is a state of ease that preserves the status quo, to the contrary, challenges beckon you out of the comfort zone and towards progress. If you choose to avoid the challenge, you are choosing to remain in a place of familiarity, which is also a place of stagnation (for example, someone who refuses to become computer literate). If avoiding the challenge is not an option, you may choose to work through it or find a way to co-exist with it to find a new balance (for example, the choice between becoming computer literate and having others do computer transactions on your behalf). In either case, a new comfort zone will be achieved, although overcoming the challenge rather than coping with it will lead to a superior state of balance. In choosing to overcome a challenge, you must venture into unfamiliar territories and situations, gain new knowledge and skills, and find new ways of applying existing competences – all in an effort to master the situation and regain control and predictability.

You must ensure that the comfort zone is a servant, rather than the master of your life. As with all things, you must learn to control your desire for the comfort zone so that it serves your well-being and that of others. As a useful servant, the comfort zone, when properly guided, will keep you productive and progressive. Daniel H. Pink, author of Drive: The Surprising Truth About What Motivates Us (Riverhead, 2009), wrote, "We need a place of productive discomfort. If you're too comfortable, you're not productive. And if you're too uncomfortable, you're not productive. Like Goldilocks, we can't be too hot or too cold."

As a master, the comfort zone will cause you to hold fiercely to your status quo, where the pull of progress and advancement cannot move you forward. It may be that such a position comes from a fixed or limiting mindset that holds a negative view of obstacles; a mindset that does not understand the value that is wrapped up in a challenge and has not grasped the value that progress will create for you and for others. Without these revelations, the comfort zone can take on the status of a god in your life, where everything that represents progress is sacrificed on its altar. It is for this reason that **people who value their comfort zone above all else will likely never discover the worth that is in them nor the value that they can bring to others.**

When the comfort zone calls the shots in a life, vision, hard work, sleepless nights, risks, perseverance, courage, hope, positive attitude, and all that's necessary for advancement will always be its casualties. When you examine these "casualties," you realize that they were, in fact, the price-tag for progress, promotion, peace, wealth, love, a happy marriage, positive influence, satisfaction, meaning, and increase. From my own experiences, I find that it is very easy to talk myself out of pursuing a good idea. After all, the obstacles are real and the arguments are compelling. However, I have come to realize that **reasons only become excuses by choice**. In other words, whether I remain in my comfort zone or step out in the face of challenges, it is completely my decision. Pursuing your career will require you to sacrifice your comfort zone – will you?

The love of the comfort zone also reveals itself in unfinished work. Sometimes work is left unfinished because completion requires venturing out of the comfort zone. This may take the form of additional effort, risks, resources, know-how, and so on. Have you ever noticed that things seem to get harder the closer you are to the end? As it is said, the darkest part of night is just before dawn.

However, **there is nothing more beautiful and satisfying than completion**. Wise King Solomon in Proverbs 12:27 says, "The lazy man does not roast what he took in hunting, but diligence is man's precious possession."[18] In this proverb, the lazy man did many things. He prepared his tools, went into the

---

[18] NKJV.

woods, faced the risks of hunting, and brought back his spoil. But when it was time to prepare his spoil for eating, he couldn't be bothered because he felt that he had done enough and had earned his relaxation. However, consider, was the purpose of his hunting to look at a dead carcass or to eat cooked meat? If the purpose of your efforts has not yet been realized, then push through the discomfort, fatigue, and challenges until "mission accomplished."

(!) **When you refuse to give up, things have a way of turning in your favour**. The "second wind" is a phenomenon in distance running whereby an athlete who is too out of breath and tired to continue suddenly finds the strength to press on at top performance with less exertion. It is believed that this occurs when athletes push past the point of pain and exhaustion to give their systems enough time to warm up and begin to use their oxygen to its fullest potential to counter the build-up of lactic acid.

This phenomenon also happens in life. Author C. Hope Clark says, *"Sometimes pursuing more common sense or lucrative income opportunity can open doors for the dream. When my novel didn't sell, I began writing freelance articles. Then I established FundsforWriters, using all the grant, contest, publisher, and market research I did for myself. A decade later, once the site thrived with over 45,000 readers, I used the research I'd glean for my readers to find an agent and sign a publishing contract...for the original novel started so long ago."* [19] This is an example of someone who did not give up on their goal at the first sign of disappointment but diversified their efforts as a way of pushing past the pain of the disappointment. In the end, they remained true to their passion and secured the help they needed to realize their dream.

(!) **If failing to leave your comfort zone buries progress, then diligence is the attitude of follow-through that unearths gifts and rewards efforts**. Examine your life for patterns of unfinished projects or goals. Examine your reasons for not completing them. It may have been the wrong timing or endeavour. However, if you notice a pattern, determine whether it was the fear of leaving the comfort zone that aborted completion.

(!) **Success in your career requires you to stretch yourself beyond your place of comfort**. Expect to do

---

[19] Brewer, Robert Lee. Writer's Market 2017 – The Most Trusted Guide to Getting Published.

this often as you advance in your career.

The Nudge Forward

"Be not afraid of growing slowly, be afraid only of standing still."
– Chinese Proverb

As a family, we ventured on a road trip that saw us driving more than one hundred hours over a three-week period. We saw magnificent sights, visited beautiful places, and connected with warm people. A most important feature of our trip was the rest-stops along our way. In fact, they were indispensable. After driving for hours, we needed those rest-stops to relieve, relax, refresh, and restore our bodies. Those stops provided parking, food and water, toilets, and space to breathe, stretch, and sleep. Looking back, we would never have realized the objectives of our road trip without those stops. They literally kept the hindrances of fatigue and sickness at bay so that we could create precious family memories to last a lifetime.

The rest-stops in life are as important as the rest-stops on a road trip. When used well, they facilitate the healthy maintenance of our body, spirit, and soul. The rest-stops in life come in the form of vacation, entertainment, sleep, play, relaxation, and anything that resets your person. **Just as the rest-stops along the road are never meant to be a final destination, neither are the rest-stops in life. As long as you remain there, you are making no progress towards your destination.** While at the rest-stops on the road trip, we were always mindful of how long we remained because we had an expected time of arrival for our next destination. In fact, we stayed only as long as we needed to re-gather our strength for the journey. Our implicit signal to proceed was the call of our next destination. The facilities were pleasant and comfortable, and we had no one signaling us to move on. Nevertheless, our desire to get to our destination was greater than our desire to enjoy the pleasantries of the rest-stops.

So it is in life; vacations, entertainment, and all forms of relaxation are necessary, but your desire to advance in your career must be greater. You must know the point where staying at a rest-stop is no longer adding value to your journey. The economist calls this scenario the point of diminishing returns. It occurs when the additional person hired increases output by fewer units than the previous person hired. At this point, the economist knows that profitability was maximized by the previous hire, and if it keeps adding people to the same amount of capital, the business will start losing money.

(!) Similarly, **you must discern the point of diminishing returns when it comes to rest and relaxation. You must know when more sleep, television, social media, and invitations are jeopardizing your quest to advance your career**. For example, studies have shown the benefits of adequate sleep but have also warned against the perils of too much sleep. This may include the risks of obesity, heart disease, and early death. Meeting your obligations to your career and life will require you to plan your time and honour your priorities. This may lead you into the uncomfortable territory of declining invitations and offers of participation, even to the point of offending others. However, take comfort in knowing that pursuing your career will come at a price to you and to others.

Equally, you must know when too little relaxation is fuelling adverse outcomes in your body, relationships, and work. The great challenge of life is balance, so it's all about finding and maintaining that sweet-spot of efficiency. **For each person, that place of balance looks different and varies with their work and the seasons of their life**. So be careful how you compare your schedule to others.

(!)

Also important is knowing when to move on to the next career opportunity. An exciting opportunity of yesterday can become the rest-stop of today when you have grown to the point where it no longer stimulates your talents. Your growth has plateaued and you begin to feel bored or stifled. This is a signal that your talents are ready for a new challenge. This can be an uncertain time, as others may question your decision to move on. You may even doubt your decision in light of the privileges of the current opportunity. However, trust your instincts. Be confident in knowing that you ran your leg of the race, and it is now time to hand over the baton.

(!) **The call of the next destination will cause you to be**

restless until you seek that which is seeking you. Choosing to remain in an opportunity that you know is no longer yours will sap your passion and productivity and begin to negatively impact those around you. When you make the decision to move on, avoid rash actions. Rather, set yourself a clear departure plan and manage the transition in a way that is fair to the assignment that you are leaving, as well as to your future livelihood.

I often advise persons who know that it is time to move on from their current position to develop an exit strategy in which they are confident. When they invest the effort to do this, it's magical to see the transformation that occurs in their attitude. Suddenly, their energy returns, and conditions they once believed were intolerable now become reasonable because their plan provided a vision for the future. A feasible exit strategy brings hope because it clearly tells you that your current situation is not the end, but is a transition period for your next opportunity. If you are seeking a career change or exploring what to do in retirement, I highly recommend the book entitled, **Your Next Career – Do What You've Always Wanted to Do by Gail Geary**. It is a very practical and informative resource to inform your career transition.

Solutions-Focused

"Minds are like parachutes, they only function when they are open." – Sir James Dewar

Focusing on solutions is a choice. The pursuit of your career will constantly require you to choose your focus. With repetition, the decision to focus on solutions will grow into a habit that stimulates the recognition of insights and opportunities that focusing on obstacles can never do. Insights are of no value to someone who is constantly ruminating over obstacles. Their worth would not be recognized when they present themselves, and they would be easily trampled by the negative mindset. **The habit of focusing on solutions builds resilience, curiosity, and positivity, which are highly desirable qualities that are sought by hiring managers, and are also strong signals for promotion**.

To show how focusing on solutions works, imagine that you spent most of your day connecting the pieces of a puzzle. The process of focusing on putting the pieces in their correct places has made you familiar with the layout and design of the picture. However, there remains one piece to complete the puzzle, which you are unable to locate. Sometime later, you come across it in another puzzle box and immediately recognize it as the missing piece. The ease of recognition was triggered by your familiarity with the pieces with which you were working.

Someone who was not working on the puzzle may be hard-pressed to recognize it as the missing piece. This is the advantage that focusing on solutions creates. **The process of finding a solution obligates you to understand the current situation so well that flashes of insight and opportunities are recognized for what they are** – the missing link, the key that fits, the open door, the answer to the question being asked.

This is likely what happened to Archimedes, an ancient Greek scientist (287-212 B.C), when he discovered the Archimedes' principle.[20] He was seeking to find a way to determine the volume of an irregular shaped object without disturbing its form. One day, as he stepped into his bath tub, he noticed that the water level rose as he got in. Given that his mind was engaged in finding a solution to the problem of volume, this occurrence triggered the insight that the water displaced by an object could be used to measure its volume. It is said that he was so excited by the insight that he ran into the streets naked, shouting "Eureka, Eureka," the Greek for "I found it, I found it." It is reasonable to say that many persons in Greece took a bath on that day, but only the mind that was focused on finding the solution to the problem of volume recognized the raised water level, as an insight.

Isaac Newton had a similar experience as he sat under an apple tree pondering the mysteries of the universe. When an apple fell from the tree, it triggered an insight on gravity. He theorized that the same force that caused the apple to fall to the ground also keeps the moon from falling toward the earth, and the earth from falling toward the sun. Many persons may have seen apples fall from a tree on that day, but only the mind that was focused on the questions of the universe was positioned to connect the dots.

---

[20] Archimedes' principle indicates that the buoyant (upward) force acting on an object is equal to the weight (downward force) of the displaced fluid. http://www.livescience.com/58839-archimedes-principle.html

In similar vein, the story of how Post-It Notes came to the market is quite interesting. It started with an error in developing an adhesive solution in 1968 at 3M International. Five years later, being aware of the quest to find a way to use this adhesive, a chemical engineer employed at the company had the flash of insight that placing the adhesive on a paper could solve his problem of continually losing the page markers in his hymnal while he sang on the church choir. He suggested to the product managers that they were using the adhesive backwards. Instead of sticking the adhesive to the bulletin board, they should "put it on a piece of paper and then we can stick it to anything."[21] The rest is history, Post-It Notes is one of the top five best-selling office supply products in the world. Again, this was an insight that was recognized in the process of thinking about a solution to a problem.

Insights come to people on a daily basis but always when their minds are focused on solutions rather than on obstacles. Insights have revolutionized the way society meet needs. Insights have created jobs, increased wealth, improved quality of life, and brought hope to many.

Focusing on obstacles is useful for the purpose of understanding the nature of the problem, which naturally leads to the door of creativity and solutions. When faced with an obstacle, instead of defaulting to negative premonitions, first act in the awareness that your response is a choice. When you habitually default to anxiety in the face of obstacles, this seamless transition to anxiety gives the appearance that you have no say in the matter. However, this is not the case. That's just how an entrenched habit works – it is effortless.

Second, identify the menu of responses available to you. This is your first act of empowerment. You could abandon your plans, find a way around it, do nothing, ask for help, etc. The very process of clearly identifying all possible responses debunks the "I have no choice" deception that precipitates a victim mentality. Third, choose to focus on the response that has the greatest potential of turning the situation in your favour. Specifically, take each option and think it through to its logical conclusion. Then choose the option that is most likely to take you to your intended goal.

Finally, dedicate your mental and other energies into making your

---

[21] Hiskey, Daven. Post-It Notes Were Invented By Accident. Today I Found Out – Feed Your Brain. http://www.todayifoundout.com/index.php/2011/11/post-it-notes-were-invented-by-accident/ (accessed October 20, 2016).

chosen option work for you. Review the situation in light of your choice, and get information and help to outline a feasible plan of action. Then, work your plans, not your fears.

The purpose of the preceding section on mindset is to raise your awareness of the decisive role that your perspectives play in your career decisions and in your life. It is said that what you are aware of you can control, and what you are not aware of controls you. It is always advantageous to be in control of your thoughts. With a mindset that is proactive, positive and poised for progress, you are well-positioned to benefit from the discussions of the chapters that follow, which will address the questions of career choice and success.

Working Past Obstacles

Points	Notes
The obstacles I face are (e.g., I have no money to pursue my certification):	
My options are (loan, bursaries, defer):	
The assumption(s) upon which each option is based (e.g., option to get loan: I must have good credit score):	
The assumption(s) I could change to make my options more feasible? (e.g., I could get someone to co-sign the loan):	
The pros and cons of each option are:	
My most feasible option is:	
I will do the following to pursue my chosen option (list steps):	
Guiding Principle: Awareness that my response is a choice.	

_____

_____

_____

_____

_____

S: Self-Awareness

"Don't ask what the world needs. Ask what makes you come alive, and go do it. Because what the world needs is people who have come alive." – Howard Thurman

It Is a Journey

(!) **The journey to finding your career begins with knowing yourself**. We each have tendencies regarding how we process information and how we act and react. These inclinations form our personalities. Becoming self-aware is one of the most transformational revelations of my life. I first came across the concept of personality types while studying a book entitled You've Got Style, by Dr. Robert Rohm. I recall the moment of enlightenment during the teachings when I thought, "Oh, so you mean that there is nothing wrong with my husband…he is just different?" This revelation came as both a relief (that nothing was wrong) and a disappointment (I wanted to be right). Back then, I sadly believed that if you were not like me, something had to be wrong with you! I was in my mid-thirties when I came across this knowledge.

As I grew in understanding myself, and by extension others, I was saddened that this kind of information is not common knowledge. In fact, it is so important that I believe it should be taught from kindergarten! In all my learning up to graduate school, no one at home, school, or in the community shared this information with me. These feelings only became stronger as my relationships improved in light of this knowledge. I felt betrayed by all my formal and informal educators (it subsequently occurred to me that perhaps they were not aware of it either). I began to beat on myself for the pain I had caused in my relationships in the wake of my ignorance of personality types.

Years later, I read an article written by Dr. Robert Rohm, who mentioned that he actually came across the knowledge of personality types in his mid-fifties. I was surprised. It then dawned on me that I had a twenty-year head-start on him. If he had learned this information in his mid-fifties and had been positively impacting so many persons, then I had better stop whining and start maximizing the use of this knowledge to both strengthen my relationships and help others.

In my first order of business, I put together a slide-show presentation and was pleased to invite my family members to share Christmas dinner and a presentation – on personality insights, of course. If you have two ears and will listen, I will share this information with you, even if you are a teddy bear! Self-awareness is that important. There are several personality models of which you may educate yourself, including *free online resources* [22] . They all point in the same direction, know thyself, and in effect, know others. If you have never come across this information, do give yourself the gift of this knowledge. Start online – the "libraries" of the world are literally at your fingertips.

In the context of your career, self-awareness matters because you are hard-wired for your purpose in life. The idea of being hard-wired for purpose has been supported by scientific research and studies that have used decades of data to predict links between personality types and career fulfilment. These research results continue to guide students in choosing post-secondary studies, new graduates in making career choices, and organizations in structuring work for maximum employee engagement.

Your personality contains clues that will guide your exploration in the treasure hunt for your career. Have you ever participated in a treasure hunt? You start with the anticipation and excitement of finding the treasure. You are in a hurry too because you want to be the first to find the prize. The

---

[22] https://www.16personalities.com/.

treasure hunt for your career is even better, as each person has their own prize waiting to be found by them. An important aspect of a treasure hunt is the clues that guide the discovery of the treasure. Good clues achieve that subtle balance between intrigue and challenge. They are engaging enough to hold your interest, yet challenging enough to fully employ your faculties in the process of leading you towards the prize. Remember that the hunt is just as precious as the prize – as the lessons of the process will help you make the most of the treasure.

(!) **Personality hard-wiring suggests that the most important career clues are written in your DNA** – hence, the importance of self-awareness in your career search. I am inspired by the medical account of the development of the foetus in the womb.[23] Starting with two cells – the egg and sperm – the fertilized egg divides into trillions of cells that each gravitate to their kind to form the organs and systems that make up the intricacies of the human body. I am energized to think that if the basic building blocks of my body, which are my cells, know how to find their place and function effectively, then certainly, I have been enabled at the individual level to find my place and effectively function in my career to meet the needs of society. **You can** (!) **use the knowledge that you are a creature of instinct to recognize and embrace** your personality and make confident decisions for your studies and career.

(!) **It is important to recognize that the journey into self-awareness is entirely reserved for human beings**. Self-awareness is the capacity to project and watch the movie of your life on the screen of your mind. You have the ability to examine your actions and motives, and assess and modify them. No animal has this ability.

Animals do, however, have personalities. I visited friends who have two beautiful Chihuahuas. One dog was infinitely open to being petted, while the other dog, though gentle, made it clear that it had its limits where petting was concerned. Animals are also quite intelligent – parrots learn to talk, horses to dance, and lions and dolphins to jump through hoops. Animals can even do some things better than humans. But despite these abilities, animals have no awareness of a "self." The Chihuahuas cannot examine their behaviour towards visitors to their masters' home and choose to

---

[23] Jakes, T. D. Instinct – The Power to Unleash Your Inborn Drive. FaithWords, 2015.

be more open or more selective about being petted. That option to examine and choose was never made available to them.

When people make comments such as, "I love the way I am," or "I hate this about me," there is a relationship between the subject, "I," and the object, "me." These statements suggest that an internal analysis occurred that involved either "a standing back from, or a projecting outwards from." This implies that there had to be an analyst and a subject. This occurrence testifies to the ability that human beings have to examine "self-in-action." **The ability to self-assess was given only to human beings, as we are the highest expression of God's creations – in His Image, or like God.**

You can use this ability to self-examine to your benefit or to your disadvantage. For the latter, you can focus on the things that you don't like to the point of frustration, inactivity, sadness, or even depression. You may equally choose to use this ability to change what you do not like, and identify and build those things that you do like. The following are examples of insightful self-awareness questions to ask in the course of finding your career path.

What Do You Care About and Do Well?

"Pleasure in the job puts perfection in the work." – Aristotle

In the context of your career, self-awareness can answer the question of, what do I care about and what do I do well? There are profound reasons why different things matter to different people. Interestingly, **the word career can be broken down into "care-er." What will you be the caretaker of in life**? What matters most to you? What occupies your thoughts? What do you enjoy doing? The answers to these questions are career clues.

Societal needs vary and each person is implicated in meeting them. It follows that we cannot all be invested in meeting the same needs. There are many things that I believe are important, such as healthcare, homeland security, geography, and so on but they do not appeal to me enough to make a career of them. What matters to me is writing, training, strategizing, encouraging, and helping people reach their goals. **Through our interests**

and style, life helps us to locate ourselves in the business of meeting needs by pointing us to the area of work where we should apply ourselves.

To benefit from this guidance, activate your ability to self-examine and begin to note the conversation topics that get you animated. Also, what are your entertainment choices, such as the types of programs that you tend to watch on television or the movies you enjoy? What do the programs have in common and what are the reasons for your likes and dislikes? Follow your spending trail. What do your receipts say matter to you – sports, books, fashion? When you consider volunteering your time, what causes or organizations come to mind? Note commonalities in your responses – for example, are your interests people or task-focused? Is there a tendency towards technical work, advocacy, creativity, or the use of numbers? There are career clues contained in the patterns that you identify.

You must also answer the question of your personality style – are you energized when you are with others or when you are alone? Are you cautious or free-spirited? Do you prefer a fast-pace or an even-pace? The answers to the questions of your interests and style represent a starting point to narrowing your career search. To demonstrate, if your interest points to the area of advocacy, that choice could be further narrowed by your tendency to be animated by issues affecting youth. Your personality inclination of being even-paced and cautious could further refine your career search by pointing you to work as a policy administrator for youth affairs, instead of a youth community mobilizer.

I have implicitly used self-awareness to guide my career, both in starting the journey and in changing directions. As an example, following completion of my graduate studies, I turned down an attractive job offer in exchange for one that paid significantly less because it seemed more in line with my interests. Somehow, the bells, whistles, and perks of the attractive job offer did not resonate with my inner passions. Even though I was criticized for my decision, I had an inner peace about it.

As I examine that decision today through a clearer lens of self-awareness, I realized that although I was not aware of it then, my decision was also based on my personality style. For instance, I have learned that I enjoy being on the frontline of results. I like to be close to where the action is happening. So even though the job offer that I rejected paid more, it played the role of facilitator of socio-economic growth, while the offer that I accepted was directly stimulating social and economic development.

Similarly, when I embarked upon a career change from organizational sustainability, I somehow instinctively looked within. I knew that work satisfaction mattered, so whatever path I chose, it had to be true to who I was and what made me tick. By soul-searching, I realized that nothing satisfied me more than helping someone realize their goals and fulfill their purpose.

I researched programs on leadership, but none seemed feasible, given my daily responsibilities. After my course search stalled, a situational clue came by way of an unsolicited email from a business school – talk about timing. As I perused the curriculum offerings, I noted a program in Human Resources Management. The content appealed to me, and equally important, the course delivery aligned with my routine. I also felt an inner nudge saying, "Go for it." As I went through the course, the content resonated with my interests, and by the end of the program, I knew I had found my calling. It now seems uncanny that I had not made the connection to Human Resources prior to then. **Sometimes career recognition is instantaneous, while at other times, it is a step-by-step process**.

Self-awareness also helps you to recognize and own the value of what you have, which then energizes you for the work. Before starting the Human Resources program, I had another situational clue that had come in the form of a job offer in Human Resources. At the time, I was grateful for the opportunity to try something different because I knew that I was ready for a change. However, I did not feel excited about the job. I now understand why this was the case – it was not yet clear to me that Human Resources appealed to my interests. As soon as I confirmed my interest in Human Resources Management through a combination of self-awareness and training, I was able to embrace the job with enthusiasm.

When you recognize your calling, it is easier to embrace the opportunities that open for the expression

of your talents, which then creates the atmosphere for their maximum use and benefit. The reverse is true – self-ignorance makes it difficult to recognize and own your talents. This makes it easy to miss the opportunities that arise to express those abilities, and sets the stage for the pearls of opportunity and talent to be trampled.

I encourage you to embark on the journey of self-awareness. I completed a certification program that uses personality styles to predict satisfying careers. You may have already guessed, the starting point of the analysis is self-awareness. There are many resources available, as well as persons and organizations that have packaged themselves to enlighten you on your interests, personality style, and talents. ***Refer to this free online resource that uses your interests to predict satisfying careers.***[24] The investment made in getting to know yourself is worth its weight in gold.

What Do Others Say You Do Well?

"The reward for work well done is the opportunity to do more."
– Jonas Salk

The people around you will also notice your personality and interests, so pay attention to what is said about your style and talents. I've learnt that **people almost always have a point.** If you are self-unaware or dismissive, then what others have to say about your abilities and style may not resonate. However, when you are operating in self-awareness, people will in general confirm what you already know and alert you to areas on unawareness. Pay particular attention to similar feedback about your style and talents from people who do not know each other, or even if they do, did not agree beforehand on what to tell you concerning your talents.

I've learned from experience that **it takes courage to receive feedback about self**. Even affirming feedback can sometimes be difficult to hear, especially in cases where insecurities are in operation. I used to take a dismissive approach to affirmation about my talents – the irony was that I lived to hear them! However, I realized that the discomfort was rooted in me

---

[24] https://www.mynextmove.org/explore/ip.

taking credit for what is ultimately not mine. Now that I see that

(!) **all affirmation truly belongs to God because all ability is from Him**, I confidently own my talents as gifts from God. Each time these gifts are affirmed, it reminds me of the privilege that I have been accorded to have the abilities of God flow through me to do good. I see it as an opportunity to be thankful and to mobilize these talents for greater good. I now listen keenly to what is being said, not for vainglory, but for further clues to better inform the meeting of needs. My talents are not about me; they never were. They are about enabling me to successfully complete my assignment on earth to help others.

If listening to affirming words can be uncomfortable, how much more listening to constructive feedback? **It takes courage**

(!) **to appreciate criticisms – so much courage that most people fail to examine them to their benefit**. Criticisms, even when meant to be constructive, are not always properly packaged or may not always be on point. However, if you believe that people are always seeing something that you are not seeing, then wisdom demands that you be open to information that may give you a clearer picture of yourself and your environment. The question, "*I believe that you are seeing something that I am not seeing. Help me to understand what you meant when you said so and so...?*" will go a long way in building relationship equity. This listening question is effective because it sends subliminal messages to others that say, "You have something important to contribute," "I am open to hearing constructive criticism," and "I have the confidence to admit fault and the willingness to improve."

(!) **To protect your mind against damaging criticism, examine all criticisms through the lens of what is true.** The truth is that you have a purpose, you have talents, and you have the power to do an amazing amount of good with the opportunities that are around you. This practice will quickly show you the criticisms that require instant dismissal, those that need to be turned inside out or upside down to be of benefit, and those that are to be taken as is.

For example, if someone were to say, "You are of no use! You are just getting in the way with all your criticisms and negative talk." By assessing this comment through the lens of truth, you would immediately dismiss the idea of being useless, as you are of immense worth. That comment was likely coming from a place of frustration and/or ignorance of your value. So for your own mental health, do quickly forgive; however, since people almost always have a point, pay attention to the idea that you are negative and getting in the way. If your intent is to criticize, it will not be appreciated. But if your intent is to be helpful, then the feedback is saying that your words are not supporting your good intentions. Choose to adjust the way in which you offer your opinions. For instance, instead of saying, "That will not work because of the cost" (which most people will interpret as opposition), adjust your statement to, "How about doing it this way to reduce the cost?" When you add a solution to your concern, people will implicitly hear that you are supportive of their efforts and want them to succeed; as a result, they will be more open to your feedback.[25] This example demonstrates the benefits of filtering feedback through the lens of truth.

With this approach, even feedback that is meant to cripple will be of benefit. For at the very least, the feedback has revealed the mind of the person, which is crucial information to inform a wise response. Examine all feedback on your personality and talents through the lens of truth. Note similarities of views, especially those that resonate with you. If you doubt what has been said, instead of being quick to rebut, invest the time to ask clarifying questions such as, "How so?" and "What are your reasons for saying that?"

(!) **Be proactive in asking others to share their opinions on what you do well and what could be improved**. I recall doing this with a manager. I was surprised at how nervous I was to solicit their opinion on an area that I could improve. However, I pressed through with the question due to my commitment to self-improvement. Interestingly enough, without hesitation, they pointed out an area for improvement. I noted the points made and placed them in the context of my personality and the environment within which I worked. In the end, I was very happy that I asked, and the feedback increased my competence and confidence in doing my job.

(!) **Do not rebut what has been said when receiving solicited feedback**. Bear in mind that the views remain the opinion of the person, and that's what you requested. Rather than expressing disagreement, ask questions to get a clearer

---

[25] Consider affirming ways to offer your opinion when you do not support a position.

understanding of what is meant. It is always useful to clarify the reasons behind the feedback, as this will help you to see yourself from the perspective of the person. An honest comment such as, "I never saw it from that perspective" will show that you are truly listening.

You are not obligated to agree with what was said, but since you asked for their views, be polite and thank them for sharing their insight. If you truly appreciate the contribution that all feedback makes to personal growth, then your gratitude will come across as sincere. Should you permit the conversation to degenerate into a debate, it may be the last straightforward feedback that you get from that person.

Your reaction to feedback sends clear messages to those around you. It is in your best interest to ensure that your signals communicate that you are comfortable with feedback. Too often, a hostile approach to criticisms (whether overt or covert) depreciates relationships, and leaves the person wandering in in the wilderness of stagnation, while they blame everyone and the kitchen sink for their predicament. If only they were open to constructive criticism, they could have addressed their limitation and enjoyed the satisfaction of progress.

On your own, you cannot be the best version of yourself. The views of others provide useful information in your quest for self-awareness. You need the insights and sharpening effect of others. Whether they do so in a pleasant manner or not, people will always seek to sharpen you with their solicited and unsolicited opinions. However, whether you improve or remain dull is your choice.

Personal Feedback Template

Action	Question/ Statement	Why
Objective for requesting feedback	For permission to act, insight on how to act, or both?	Provides context for processing responses
Sample feedback questions	* What could I do differently to advance...? * Where could I dedicate more attention...? * How could I improve the situation...?	People tend to be uncomfortable pointing out personal weaknesses, so craft your questions carefully
Ask listening questions to clarify doubts or concerns	How so? What are your reasons for saying that?	To see things from the perspective of the person
Ask for suggestions	What would you suggest if you were in my place?	Identifies options
Express genuine gratitude for feedback	Thank you for your insights	Leaves door open for future insights
Guiding principle: People are always seeing something that you are not seeing.		

_____

_____

_____

_____

What if You're Not Aware of Your Talents?

"For the things we have to learn before we can do them, we learn by doing them." – Aristotle

People sometimes grew up in situations that dismissed their value and negatively compared them to others. Such experiences can serve to bury talents. If you relate to this scenario, it is time to unearth your talents. At the beginning of the book, I referred to the innate abilities that humans have to meet needs. However, if you are in doubt of having a talent or not certain what it is, start somewhere that will give you an opportunity to prove the answer for yourself. Put a stake in the ground, so to speak – everything requires a starting point. Anchor your stake at a place that will give you the greatest opportunity to prove the answer to the question of your talent. **Just as eating will prove that food satisfies, doing things will prove the talents you possess**. Start by doing something that is in line with an issue that you care about, or at the very minimum, doing something that is at hand to be done – just DO something.

This approach is also useful for someone who is talented in many things and feels challenged to commit to an area. If someone asks you for help, go right ahead and help. In the process, you might find that you actually enjoyed the activity or maybe not at all. Either way, you would have learned something more about yourself. These opportunities serve as situational clues that will help to guide you to finding your career.

I never knew that I would enjoy teaching until I agreed to help with presenting lessons at the children's classes at church. Over time, I moved on to teaching teens and then adults. This realization has figured into my career as a presenter, facilitator and keynote speaker. Doing something may also reveal what is not for you. A friend shared how after agreeing to work with his Dad in his contracting business over the summer, his father pulled him aside on the second day and offered him the option to quit. It was clear to both that the work of a contractor was not his thing. He did in fact quit and is now an accomplished veterinarian (credit to the Dad for acting in the best interest of his son rather than his business). That is the power of doing something – it uncovers and reveals.

Doing something has a way of uncovering career clues that would never show themselves without effort. **Attempting something can** ⊙ **reveal your love or dislike for a vocation, as well as give you a clearer understanding of yourself**. These are all clues to discovering your career, which you uncovered by your decision to try. Discovering your career can sometimes be like a multiple choice exam. Some answers you may know intuitively, while others you may arrive at through a process of elimination. Either way, getting to the answer is what matters.

⊙ **Before investing substantial resources in an area for which you are uncertain, start in the capacity of helping someone with a task or job shadowing for a time**. The experience will provide insight and useful clues to guide your career search. Common practice shows that people who take a positive approach to life by stepping out and trying tend to move ahead and achieve more, and are richer, happier, and healthier than persons who take a negative approach to life. So go ahead, try something to advance your career.

Power Perspective for Self-Awareness

What if you were to embrace the perspective that says, *"The security of my career lies in my innate abilities, rather than in a job"?* This view immediately keeps the accountability for your career progress with you, instead of passing it to something (job) or someone (employer) else. By transferring this accountability, you are also diminishing your power to take control of your career. Your focus shifts from developing your talents and keeping them current in order to meet the changing demands of the labour market to focusing on how to get and keep a particular job. So, even as you develop your talents for a particular job, the idea that your security lies in your job can operate like blinkers that may cause to you to ignore important elements of the changing skill requirements in an increasingly dynamic labour market.

To nurture a resilient mindset, I propose that you embrace the idea of income security (instead of job security). Today's reality of rapidly changing consumer demands that fuel changing skills demands increasingly renders the idea of job security obsolete. In fact, I believe that what is referred to as "job security" has always been "income security" – the former term being the "face" of the latter. The advantage of thinking in terms of "income security" is that it pre-disposes the mind to think more broadly about career; specifically, to habitually review ways in which you can create income streams by continually monitoring and updating your expertise to meet changing market demands.

(!) Equally important is recognizing that **your ability to meet needs is inalienable; that is, you are one with your talents**. Consequently, a notice of job termination from an employer is really saying that they can no longer afford to pay you to meet the needs of their clients, within their current operating context. This in no way means that your expertise was also terminated. If you were capable of providing IT support before you lost your job, you are still capable of doing the same after the job-loss. As a result, your focus should be to either find another employer who can pay you for your expertise, find your own clients, or retool your skills to meet changing client service needs.

As stated at the beginning of the book, needs do not go into recession. What changes is how needs are met. I recall reading about a food produce company that expanded during a recession because it understood this principle. With falling consumer income and people still needing to eat, they diversified into offering "no-embellishment" produce at affordable prices. It is for the same reason that dollar stores also expanded during the recession – consumers substituted cheaper goods for more expensive brands to meet their ever-present consumption needs.

Unwelcome news of a job-loss is difficult to process, especially because it touches our ability to provide for our basic needs. (!) That said, **guard against the temptation to permit disappointment to cause you to marginalize and ignore your abilities**. When the job outlook seems bleak, rather than losing faith in your ability to meet needs, consider options for repackaging and repositioning your talents. Remember, (!) **talents are like seeds – the more of the right care that is given to them, the greater the yield**. If you are experiencing difficulty landing a job, assess whether your packaging is misaligned; that is, whether your skills require updating or your personality or attitude is limiting (we will address the question of personality later in the book).

Summarizing Self-Awareness

(!) Self-Awareness is the foundation for career building because it embodies personal career clues that are contained in your interests and personality, as well as in your talents and abilities. Given that you are a creature of instinct, be confident in your decisions to use those clues to choose a career path. Remain open to trying new things and dedicate yourself to the self-discovery that comes with the process of doing. Value all your experiences and assess them with awareness – the opportunities that come your way, the connections that you make, or the challenges that you face. Each one will bring you useful information to chart your course forward. The key is to assess, instead of to dismiss or resent them. Be committed to personal growth – everyone is a work-in-progress.

I encourage you to complete the checklist below to have an overall profile of your personality, interests, and concerns. This information will help you to plan your next steps towards clarifying and/or pursuing your career goals.

With a clearer understanding of yourself, you are now ready to examine the next step of career exploration, that of relating your personality, talents, and interests to the world in which you live.

Self-Awareness Checklist

Points	Notes
My personality type results say (www.16personalities.com):	
The things that interest me are:	
I come alive when I am:	
My career profile interest results say (www.mynextmove.org/explore/ip):	
Things I would do if I faced no obstacles are:	
My reasons for being uncertain about my career decisions are:	
My next steps to move closer to my career goals are:	

_____

_____

_____

_____

_____

E: Environment–Awareness

"Don't go around saying the world owes you a living, it owes you nothing – it was here first." – Mark Twain

Where Do You Live and What's Happening There?

(!) **Your ability to meet needs must relate to the time in which you live.** Now that you are more aware of your interests and personality style, it is time to relate them to the world in which you live. The key questions to ask are, where do I live and what is happening there? You are alive today to meet the needs of today, not the needs of 150 years ago nor those of 150 years to come. Even if you are a planner, you are planning now because society needs to plan today for tomorrow. **Notice the things that are happening around you. Look around** (!) **you with awareness and purpose to see consumer needs and employment trends**.

Starting with yourself, examine the things you do on a daily basis and note the products and services that you use to get those things done. For example, you will likely sleep on a bed, eat food, wear clothes, communicate, travel in private or public transport to get to appointments, and so on. Take the time to list these activities, along with the implicated products and services – the list could go on and on. This exercise is meant to highlight how your needs give rise to the existence of businesses/ organizations, as many professions are mobilized to enable you to complete your daily routine – builders, furniture makers, farmers, fashion designers, information technologists, automobile makers, and many others (see examples in table below). Now multiply the impact of your individual needs by the population in your city, and you will get an idea of the magnitude and type of needs to be met in your community.

Needs Give Rise To Careers

Daily activities	Products/People	Careers
Eat	Food, servers, ...	Farming, hospitality, ...
Sleep	Bed, linen, ...	Carpentry, design, ...
Travel, etc.	Car, roads, ...	Auto industry, planning, ...
...	...	...

Take note of consumer trends and demands when you listen to the news and read journals and articles. Which industries are growing and which ones are declining? Note the reasons for the growth or decline. When the construction industry is booming, for example, it generates work for builders, as well as for trades-people. My husband called a plumber to unclog our kitchen sink. He came with the right tools and got the job done quickly. He used his cell phone to process the credit card payment; and while there, he received two calls, presumably for other jobs. He was done and on his way in less than 30 minutes. I admired the seamless process. He was organized, effective and efficient, and up-to-date with technology. When I consider all the new housing developments in my community, and the needs of home-owners, it is easy to extrapolate that there will be enough work to keep him gainfully employed.

Consider the service methods that are becoming obsolete and the ones that are emerging? These answers will provide valuable information for predicting the outlook for careers that will be in-demand. **Automation and artificial intelligence are key factors that will be impacting jobs over the next two decades**, especially jobs that include repetitive tasks and computations (e.g., jobs in apparatus assembly and finance). Some of the jobs that are least likely to be automated are in teaching, family medicine, and engineering[26].

Being aware of your environment to identify career opportunities also includes listening to your frustrations, as well as those of others towards products, processes, and services. What are people complaining about? Is it inadequate or limited service options? The distinction will help to identify growing demand for a service or to diversify delivery of a particular service. **Recognize that product or service complaints are really people asking for something they need and for which they are likely willing to pay to have access**. I read about a cleaning company that started from a couple's discontent with available home cleaning options. When they contacted existing services, they found limited offerings that did not meet their needs. So guess what? They started their own home cleaning business that has since grown across Canada.

In another example, my home city of Ottawa, Canada, gets lots of snow over the winter period. It is common for home owners to contract a snow-removal service provider for the winter. The amount of snowfall usually decides who gets the better side of the contract (homeowner or service provider). Then I heard a snow-ploughing on-demand service being advertised. I immediately thought, here is someone who has listened to the needs of people because not everyone who wants to have their snow removed, requires the service for the entire winter.

I signed some documents using an electronic signature application. It was as easy as a few clicks of my computer mouse. I compared it to the previous process that required me to print the documents, sign, scan, and email them to the next signatory, who would have to go through the same process. As I enjoyed the ease of the new process, I paused with a smile on my face in appreciation of the person(s) who went further than seeing a problem to actually applying their resources and talents to developing a more efficient process. I also hoped that they were enjoying adequate financial returns on their decision to invest in a solution.

The point of the previous examples is to stimulate your thinking on how careers are created. You may be rationalizing that you have

---

[26] MacFarland, Janet. Will Your Job Go Extinct? Find Out How Precarious Your Profession Is. The Globe and Mail. http://www.theglobeandmail.com/report-on-business/economy/jobs/what-risk-does-automation-pose-to-your-job/article30434394/ (accessed April 9, 2017).

no desire to be an entrepreneur so none of the preceding applies to you (I will examine this idea towards the end of this chapter). Not so fast! In fact, this mentality applies across the board, even to employees. **Whether you are an employee or an entrepreneur, your ability to correctly identify and meet the needs of your clients will determine your success**.

If you consistently and effectively meet your clients' needs, in no time, opportunities for promotion will seek you. Managers note feedback (especially unsolicited) from their clients on the work of their employees. With consistently positive comments from clients and peers, these employees are more likely to earn awards and recognition.

An intuitive employee views clients' complaints as a call for innovation. This is one of the secrets of successful people, whether in the workplace of in business. They understand that **often, the call to innovate manifests as an unmet need clothed in a complaint**. Given the limitations of your position, you may not always be able to give clients what they want; nonetheless, an intuitive listening ear will pre-dispose you to finding solutions that could at least improve their situation. If you choose to invest your efforts into meeting the unmet needs of your clients, you are well underway to a promotion and increased income. This approach will, of necessity, require you to go the extra mile, invest extra time, and leave your comfort zone. However, such is the price of growth and progress.

What Are the Demographic Trends Around You?

"We pay attention to every demographic in every country, so we are going to focus on building things that teens are going to like, and we are also going to focus on building things that other folks are going to like." – Mark Zuckerberg, CEO of Facebook

The existence of people guarantees needs. Demography is the study of changes in the number of births, marriages, deaths, etc. in a particular area during a period of time.[27] Demographic trends are the foundation factors that guarantee your career because every service or product is ultimately about people. Population changes in your community and beyond provide insights into the types of needs that people have and the

---

[27] Cambridge English Dictionary.

outlook for careers that will be implicated in meeting those needs. The following excerpt from the Canadian Medical Association in its September 2016 report, The State of Seniors Health Care in Canada, is an example of one demographic trend that Canada and other developed countries are facing: *Statistics Canada reports that over 15% of our population at the last census was over 65; it was 7.6% in 1960. For the first time there are more people aged 65 and older than there are children aged 0-14 years. Based on population projections the share of Canadians 65 and older will continue to rise and that by 2024 they will account for 20.1% of the population. By 2036 seniors are expected to make up 25% of the population. People aged 85 years and over make up the fastest growing age group in Canada — this portion of the population grew by 127% between 1993 and 2013. Statistics Canada projects, based on a medium-growth scenario, there will be over 62,000 Canadians aged 100 and older by 2063.*

The preceding information addresses the impact of Baby Boomers (persons born between 1946 and 1964) as a demographic group. This group represented a population growth spurt that started after the Second World War. The needs of this group generate demands for enhanced succession planning as they retire from the workplace, retirement living services (real estate, entertainment, leisure, etc.), health care, estate planning and management services, and end-of-life services.

Immigration is another demographic trend of significance in Canada, where over 250,000 newcomers are welcomed annually. Again, consider the needs of this group – resettlement services, housing, language services, jobs, training, and so on. Do any of the needs of these or other demographic groups appeal to your interests? **You can analyze any demographic group to assess career opportunities**.

As you note the specific needs of each demographic group, pay particular attention to the needs that appeal to your interests and talents. Whether your life's work will lead into entrepreneurship, the not-for-profit sector, government or private enterprise, your decision should be based on the alignment of your interests and talents with the needs that are around you. Remember, **your presence on planet earth represents a deposit, and your decision to apply yourself to meeting the needs of society completes the payment.**

Demographic Trends and Needs

Demographic group	Growth trend	Needs	Career
Children	Declining	Day-care, ...	Child-care, ...
Youth	Steady	Career-guidance, ...	Counselling, ...
Seniors, etc.	Increasing	Leisure activities, ...	Event planning, ...

_____

_____

_____

_____

_____

What Are the Skills-in-Demand?

At the end of the day, the true value proposition of education is employment." – Sebastian Thrun

Educate yourself on the skills trends of government and enterprise. North America is facing the double-jeopardy of an over-supply or labour and an under-supply of required skills. The following excerpt captures the situation in Canada: *The majority of students apply to post-secondary institutions with their future careers in mind. This is especially true for those who attend college. Unfortunately, students today make decisions about their post-secondary field of study and future careers with inadequate information about what occupations will be in high demand when they graduate. As a result, some industries have too many students focusing on them, while other sectors, such as The STEM (Science, Technology, Engineering, Mathematics) – based occupations and the skilled trades face skills shortages. These shortages have been identified by the Canadian Chamber of Commerce as one of the top barriers to competitiveness.*[28] The report further stated, *One study found that one out of three Canadian graduates were in careers unrelated to their education. Unfortunately, students are attracted to programs that are superficially appealing, but which offer no simple path into jobs that are in demand.*

A similar scenario is playing out in the United States of America. In an article entitled, "U.S. Employers Have Too Much Available Labour, Not Enough Available Talent," Sunny Ackerman, the vice president and general manager of Manpower U.S. is quoted saying, *"Technology, shorter product cycles, shifting consumer demand, and new ways of working all mean that the jobs employers need done are evolving, and they need people with different skills to do them. We've found that even where there is a ready supply of labor, there isn't always a ready supply of skills. In many ways, the growing talent shortage reflects an issue of quality versus quantity. The challenge is finding people with the right skills and experience to do the work."* [29] The article further stated that, *"As the workforce shifts toward more technical and skills-based jobs, businesses are becoming more efficient and eliminating older roles while creating new ones. As a result, employers are struggling to keep up with their changing skills needs."*

[28] Human Resources Professional Association (HRPA) Report 2016. Strengthening Ontario's Workforce for the Jobs of Tomorrow.

[29] Lindzon, Jared. Fast Company – The Future of Work. https://www.fastcompany.com/3064834/the-future-of-work/us-employers-have-too-much-available-labor-not-enough-available-talent (accessed November 06, 2016).

This is a challenge that can only be addressed by a timely flow of accurate information between employers and the labour force. Equally important is having employers and employees who are equipped to give and receive on-the-job training. As Ackerman puts it, *"Employability—the ability to gain and maintain a desired job—no longer depends on what you already know, but on what you are likely to learn."*

To avoid being a victim of this mismatch of skills and needs, it is important to understand the distinction between talents and skills. Although often used interchangeably, **a talent is an ability or aptitude to do something well. A skill represents a particular application of a talent**. When we say that a person is highly talented, it means that they have a high level of aptitude for a particular task, usually indicating that they do it with ease and of a relatively higher quality than most. For example, a person who has a talent to process information very well may decide to apply it to law, psychotherapy, or mass communications. In each case, we can say that the person is a skilled lawyer, therapist, or communicator. The point here is to grasp the essence of your talent rather than being locked into the application of it (i.e., the skillset). In my case, the essence of my talent is communication, whether through writing, speaking, strategizing, or creating. My skillsets are applied through keynote speaking, training, coaching, articles, books, products, etc.

Your talent can be applied to many areas and in ever-changing ways. **It is quite acceptable and even realistic to sunset a skillset, but it is never wise to give up on your talent.** In other words, hold tightly to your talents but be flexible with your skillset. For example, if you are a talented writer and the employment outlook for writers is weak, study the market trends for writing communications and find innovative ways to adapt your writing skills to the market trends. Instead of being consumed by the idea of writing the next best-seller, examine options for blogging, writing articles or commentary for a magazine, writing speeches and documents, or creating scripts for theatre or cinema. These options could also pave the way to making your dream book a reality.

Recognize also that consumption patterns drive the demand for skills. The next time you desire the latest version of a product or service, connect the dots that it is these very desires that dinosaur current skillsets. Consequently, align your talents and interests to the skillsets of consumption trends and needs. For example, the rise of robotics and artificial intelligence is generating demand for skills in coding and design. Overall, continual learning is integral to being employable.

Certain countries have been identified as doing a good job of preparing their available talent to meet employers' skill requirements. Germany quickly comes to mind, as they have a highly developed system of partnership between government, teaching institutions, and industry that uses programs such as apprenticeships to meet skills demands. North America is lagging in this area. The Canadian Human Resources Professional Association has consistently called for the establishment of a better information infrastructure to capture current and emerging skills trends so students and employers can make more informed employment decisions.

Until that time arrives, take control of your career by being proactive in identifying employment trends from established sources[30], as well as from your knowledge of consumption trends. **Examine news and current events through the lens of skills-in-demand. Channel your energies into conducting your own research, take advantage of opportunities to share your findings in whatever forum that is at your disposal** – your family, class, school, social media, and so on. Do not despair – instead, take control of your career decisions by apprising yourself of accurate and current information.

Connect Your Interests to Needs

"Life's most persistent and urgent question is: "What are you doing for others?" – Dr. Martin Luther King Jr.

Proactivity remains the most powerful tool for advancing in your career, and it is equally effective when connecting your interests to the needs around you. When you have availed yourself of self-awareness and you are continually assessing the needs in your environment, it becomes easier to

---

[30] Canadian Labour Market Information – https://www.jobbank.gc.ca/explorecareers.do and U.S. Labour Market Information – https://www.bls.gov/k12/students.htm (accessed August 1, 2017).

recognize opportunities that speak to your interests. The following are examples of how people like you connected their interests to meeting the needs around them:

I enjoy reviewing the nominations for the annual CNN Heroes Award, which features people who are moved to action by the needs that arouse their concern. Take the case of Derreck Kayongo, a native of Uganda, who started the Global Soap Project in 2009. The group recycles partially used hotel soaps and sends them to impoverished nations as a way of fighting against infant mortality caused by lack of basic sanitation. The idea was sparked by Kayongo's experience staying in a hotel in the United States. He noted that fresh soap was brought to his hotel room daily even though the existing ones were unfinished. He said, "I tried to return the new soap to the concierge since I thought they were charging me for it. When I was told it was just hotel policy to provide new soap every day, I couldn't believe it. But I just started to think, 'What if we took some of this soap and recycled it, made brand new soap from it and then sent it home to people who couldn't afford soap?' " [31]

As a result of Kayongo's efforts to do something to address this situation, hundreds of hotels across the United States now send tons of used soap to his project for sanitizing, packaging, and distributing across the globe to people in need of this basic commodity. This is a classic example of self-awareness (knowing what interests him) meeting environment-awareness (identifying the needs around him) to inform action. No doubt his past experiences and knowledge contributed to his decision – first-hand knowledge of the lack of soap and its impact on people, as well as his knowledge of the soap business from his father, who was a former soap maker.

Home Depot is another example. The founders, Bernard Marcus and Arthur Blank, were both fired from their jobs due to a corporate power struggle. Being avid do-it-yourselfers (DIYers), over coffee one day they dreamed up the idea of a superstore that would offer a huge variety of home improvement merchandise at great prices, along with a highly trained staff. Employees would not only be able to sell, they would also be able to walk customers at every skill level through almost any home repair or improvement.

---

[31] Ruffins, Ebonne. Recycling hotel soap to save lives. CNN Heroes 2011. http://www.cnn.com/2011/US/06/1/cnnheroes.kayongo.hotel.soap/index.html (accessed October 20, 2016).

Three months after this conversation, they incorporated the business, and with help from others, opened the first two Home Depot stores in Atlanta the following year in 1979. [32] The company grew to over two thousand stores, and hired over three hundred thousand employees. Their story confirms the power of the interest-environment combination. Their interest and experience in home improvement, as well as in retailing, positioned them well to assess the market conditions. They saw the needs-gap – existing home improvement stores did not offer the array of services that would make it easy for DIYers to get their projects done. Thus, they developed a business model that met the needs of DIYers, including providing DIY workshops free of cost to customers.

There is also the story of Carla Jackson, 2015 Louisiana State Teacher of the Year. In an article entitled, "Why I Became a Teacher? It Was My Destiny!," she explains what happened on that extraordinary day when she agreed to help her friend for a day in her first grade class. When she entered the classroom, most of the students ran to her to find out more about her. Her attention was drawn to a girl who seemed shy and was trying to avoid attracting attention. This immediately reminded her of childhood experiences of loss that had left her withdrawn and feeling like her wings were clipped at that age.

In Carla's words, "In that one day, I saw innocence, adventure, creativity, love, potential, eagerness, inspiration and so much more. I was engulfed with an overwhelming feeling of awe. These children turned on a light for me. I knew I had to be a part of this magical experience every day of my life. There was absolutely no question of what I was to do next. The following day, I changed my major (from engineering) to elementary education, and I have never looked back." [33] In Carla's case, even though she was on another path, an experience revealed a need that she had no idea she was so passionate to meet. This supports the point that being open to doing positive things is always profitable, as the experience may awaken or reveal dormant interests and talents of which you may not have become aware in the absence of that experience.

When talking to people who are satisfied in their career, they will likely have interesting stories as to how they got to where they are.

---

[32] The Home Depot. The Home is Where Our Story Begins. https://corporate.homedepot.com/about/history (accessed October 9, 2016).

[33] Jackson, Carla Z. Why I Became a Teacher? It Was My Destiny! Source Teaching and Learning. http://www.advanc-ed.org/source/why-i-became-teacher-it-was-my-destiny (accessed November 09, 2016).

In some cases, it was the needs around them that sparked the interest to act, while in other cases, it was the interest that led to the identification of the need.

In my own journey, I was not always certain what I wanted to pursue as a career. As a result, I used the clues within and around me as a guide. In high school, my friends were on a path to careers in the natural sciences. While I do not recall having a desire to pursue that path, I believe strongly that peer pressure would have led me there. However, in the tenth grade, the year prior to choosing my specialization, it seemed like overnight I began to struggle in one of my science courses. With the uncertainty of success in the subject, I started taking business courses and realized that I thoroughly enjoyed the study of Economics, which I pursued to graduate school. This certification opened the opportunity for me to apply my talents and skills to meeting the need for social and economic empowerment through project development and implementation.

I am not suggesting that struggling in a course is a signal to abandon its pursuit; rather, it could be an invitation to master it! Had I been certain that I wanted a career in the natural sciences, I would likely have applied myself to succeeding in that subject. However, the key point is to remain open to trying new things during career exploration, as you may never know which area will satisfy your career longings.

(!) **Embrace the occurrences in your life**. The people you meet and by whom you are inspired, as well as the opportunities that you pursue. They all provide clues that are useful in pointing you to your career. So journey through these experiences with the awareness that each occurrence carries a useful career signal. Avoid any tendency to be nonchalant, frustrated, disappointed, or anxious.

Power Perspective for Environment-Awareness

What if you were to embrace the perspective that says, *"It is my responsibility to guarantee my own work?"* This thought may appear daunting on the surface, as most people prefer to get paid to do a job instead of being an entrepreneur. However, whether as an entrepreneur or an employee, the idea of guaranteeing your own work can be applied in a profitable way.

People have differing risk tolerances, so not everyone will be entrepreneurs in the common sense of the word. Some people are more risk-averse, which makes them better suited as employees. (!) That said, I've heard it said that **people don't really work for others; in effect, they work for themselves**. This is explained by the truism that you will reap the fruits of whatever decisions and attitudes you bring to your job. If you work with diligence, you are likely to get promoted. Conversely, if you work slothfully, promotions will pass you by or you may even lose your job. In essence, this perspective makes everyone an entrepreneur as each worker guarantees their own job by earning the right to keep, advance, or lose it. The question, therefore, is not whether you are an employee or an entrepreneur but whether you are a frontline or back-office entrepreneur.

As a frontline entrepreneur (in the common use of the word), you assume the full risks of acquiring, organizing, and managing resources to deliver products and/or services. This requires a high level of risk-tolerance and a keen sense of how to read the needs and trends of the market to keep your business profitable and growing. Apple, for example, did a better job than BlackBerry in anticipating and meeting the communication needs of consumers, and the results show in their respective market share and profitability.

As a back-office entrepreneur, an employee does not normally assume the capital risks of a frontline entrepreneur. However, no matter their level within the organization, **if an employee believes that they are responsible for guaranteeing their job, they** (!) **will keep their fingers on the pulse of the changing needs of their clients and use their influence to ensure that their organization's product or service remains relevant**.

For example, imagine that you are a client service agent. Your job places you in daily contact with users of your company's products. Firstly, recognize that this is an advantage of your job that neither your manager nor the CEO of the organization possess.[33] You note that customers tend to complain about a particular product feature. Thinking like a worker, you may do your best to address

---

[33] The show, *Undercover Boss*, seeks to compensate for the disadvantages that CEOs/ managers face in their position of often being distanced from the users of their product/ service.

or explain the limitations, or even offer perks. However, thinking like an entrepreneur would require you to communicate this concern upwards and propose solutions to your management, as feasible. For this approach to succeed, your immediate and middle managers would all have to adopt the same entrepreneurial thinking by ensuring that your feedback is addressed.

An employee who operates from this mindset within their organization will likely increase business, secure their job, command higher compensation, and attract promotions. **Whether organizationally or individually, work is guaranteed by decisions that anticipate and meet the needs of clients**. Pursue staying power with your work. That is, continually seek to make your product or service so useful to others that they cannot fathom living without it. Such a perspective keeps an entity relevant and profitable, and an employee proactive and empowered for their employer and for themselves.

As you nurture an entrepreneurial mindset (even as an employee), you will not be intimidated by the realities of change, whatever the origin, because, through daily practice, you have become adept at reading your "market", anticipating the needs of clients, and responding accordingly. This ability will make you confident in using your expertise at any time, in any place, and at any stage in your life – even in the retirement years.

Summarizing Environment-Awareness

As you pursue your career, be aware and intentional. Examine news with the intent to identify consumer trends and needs, as well as the ways in which work is changing due to automation and artificial intelligence. Note significant demographic movements and the emerging needs of specific groups. Connect your interests to needs around you by examining the prospects for work in your areas of interest. As an employee, no matter your level in your organization, embrace an entrepreneurial mindset by using your position to provide service that consistently meets the needs of your clients.

Whether chicken or egg, **it's the coming together of self-awareness and environment-awareness that fertilizes a career choice.** With gestation in the womb of training and preparation, you will birth and enjoy a successful career that brings satisfaction to you and to others. The next chapter will examine how to prepare yourself for the market once you have a fair idea of the career you want to pursue.

Environment-Awareness Checklist

Points	Notes
Complaints you hear/have about products and services:	
Complaints of interest to you:	
Changes that could be made to address those complaints:	
Industries that are growing and declining:	
Skills in demand and decline:	
Significant demographic trends:	
Needs generated by demographic trends:	
Skills demand of government and business:	

T: Trained Talents and Personality

"Do not neglect the gift that is in you" 1 Timothy 4:14a NKJV.

Bring Out the Best in Yourself

Now that your interests, personality, and the needs around you are coalescing in a particular direction, it is time to develop your inborn talents and put them to work to meet needs. **If your career is a wheel, then training is the factor what causes it to turn. Training brings together the two aspects of self-awareness and environment-awareness through the process of preparation**. Training enables you to bring your ability to the marketplace, where you can be paid to meet needs. The training process is its own reward in that it comes with the inalienable compensation of knowledge and expertise gained. This no one can take from you, except that you choose to marginalize, devalue, or ignore it.

Training acknowledges that talents and personality are often "diamonds in the rough" that require refinement, direction, and buffing in order to provide maximum value. I recall the first time I saw a piece of raw gold in a museum display. I was taken aback because it looked like a black pebble. I thought how easily I would have discarded it as useless had I seen it lying on the ground. However, the process of refinement makes it into the desirable metal that people are willing to pay significant amounts of money to acquire and proudly use for adornment and display.

The difference between a "black pebble" (raw gold) and a beautiful golden ring is processing. So it is with your talents and personality. To bring out the best in them, you must train your talents to develop competence for the job and train your personality to embrace a positive attitude towards your work. Before examining both of these aspects, let's address the inherent value of your talent and personality.

Are Talents Equal?

For God shows no partiality [undue favor or unfairness; with Him one man is not different from another]. Romans 2:11. Amplified Version.

Marcus Buckingham and Curt Coffman, in their summary, *First, Break All the Rules – What the World's Greatest Managers Do Differently,* define talent as simply a recurring pattern of thought, feeling or behaviour. After in-depth interviews of over 80,000 managers, they conclude that all roles require talent. They suggest that it is a myth for managers to think that some roles are so easy, they don't require talent or that anyone can do a particular job.

(!) **Talents are equal in essence and substance because they all have the capacity to meet needs, and when a need is met, the common outcome is satisfaction.** To explain, one may generally rate the ability of a life guard to save lives higher than the ability of a writer to organize information. However, if a person is nowhere near water but needs to organize their business idea to present to the bank for financing, a lifeguard is of no use to them in that moment. Someone who is talented in writing a business proposal will be of more value to them just then.

(!) This example underscores the point that **it is ultimately the need at hand that determines the value of a talent.** Consequently, since different talents are required to meet different needs, it means that whatever your talent, in essence, it stands equally among all talents. It is important to grasp this truth in order to avoid the pitfall of devaluing the talents that you have and diminishing the extent to which they can be of benefit by forfeiting their development.

How often have you heard someone negatively compare

themselves with others, such as in the following example – "All I can do is to make people feel good about themselves, while you on the other hand, are so intelligent and talented in Mathematics." That person may even be you. Before you go off wallowing in self-pity and believing that God has dealt you "a bad hand," you should consider the power that is vested in your ability to make people feel good about themselves. By embracing this talent as valuable, you could consider several careers requiring this talent, such as counselling, client service, coaching, and leading people. I read about a man who successfully led a group of scientists to accomplish important work even though he knew nothing about science. He accomplished this feat because he knew how to make people feel good about themselves, which is the key to motivating people for excellence.

Look around you – many people are struggling with low self-esteem. Your talent of making others feel good about themselves can lead people to accomplish great things and may even save lives. Be aware that any dissatisfaction you may have about your talent is really your way of saying that God gave you something sub-standard (and this may not be how you really feel). So think critically before devaluing your talent.

God makes no mistakes in what He apportions to us, and everything that He gives is good. You and I are hard-wired for our purpose, so your talents were endowed to you with your purpose in mind. From The Parable of the Talents, note that the servant who got two talents did not complain that the first servant got five talents. Instead, he worked to increase that which he was given. However, the servant with the one talent fell into the trap of devaluing the talent he had, which inevitably led to the downward spiral of no training, no use, and eventual loss of his endowed position of worth in society.

(!) **Granted that talents are equal in essence, disparities in recognition and compensation may be accounted for by the way in which talents are developed and marketed.** From the previous chapter, recall the distinction between a talent and a skill, where I highlighted that a skill is the particular application of a talent. The job market compensates for skills, and there are two main factors that determine how skills are compensated. One is the skill-level required to do a job. For example, the difference in intensity of training required to become an astronaut versus that of a book-keeper will result in higher pay to the astronaut.

The other main factor is the interaction between the forces of supply and demand for the skill in question. If the demand for a skill is high and there are few qualified people, then the compensation for that job will be higher, and vice-versa. For example, if there is a high demand for trades-people and few people are qualified to work in this area, then people will pay more to attract the few available trades-people to their job.

The point of the preceding section is to encourage you to value your talent. **Any devaluing of your talent will cause you to suppress your authenticity, which is the well from which success flows**. Instead, focus your efforts on identifying and developing the skills that emanate from your talent, and that are in demand.

Recognizing Talents and Interests

Things I like to Do	Related Talent	Skills I Could Develop
Play sports	Physical agility, ...	Speed, coaching, ...
Make clothes	Creativity, ...	Sewing, designing, ...
Research ideas	Attention to detail, ...	Investigating, inventing...

_____

_____

_____

_____

(!) **Parents can play a key role in guiding career choices by supporting and nurturing the talents and interests of their children, and helping them acquire the right information on the realities of the job market**. Sometimes parents sabotage their support because of their own career preferences, fear of inadequate compensation and recognition, among other reasons. This can lead to discontent, confusion, and even despair in children, and may contribute to disengagement within the labour force at the societal level.

Like most parents, your intentions are good; so remove the fear factor from your parental guidance and take the position of an ally for the talents and interests of your children. **Empower** (!) **your children by keeping an open mind to their career decisions, acknowledging that the beaten path is not the only path to their success.** Help your child identify the various ways in which they can use their talents, as well as the market demand and trends for the areas in which they have an interest. **Like a coach, continually bring pertinent** (!) **career information to their attention and engage them in discussions on how they can best benefit others with their talents**. When your child believes that you are their career ally and not their adversary, they will be more comfortable exploring their ideas with you and more open to your feedback. Your aim should be to guide your child to develop skills that are true to their talents and interests, and to help them to gainfully bring their talents to the marketplace.

A well-respected celebrity hair-stylist shared how she would sneak her friends into her home after school to style their hair. When her mother caught on to what she was doing, she had her enrolled in beauty school. This mother saw her daughter's natural interest and talent and nurtured them by investing in training for her development. I also read about a young man who had a passion for farming. In this case, his parents did not support his career interest. Instead, they pressured him into becoming a lawyer. Thankfully, the story had a happy ending. After graduating from law school, he moved to the countryside, bought a farm, and provided legal representation to farmers.

Sometimes the desire to please parents can cause children to pursue careers that leave them feeling stuck and depressed about their future. The most dispirited case I came across is that of a student pursuing a career that has been prescribed by loving parents out of deep concern for their financial security. The cruel irony is that a job offer in this "dreaded"[34] field was secured in their first year of university. It was hard to listen to them express sadness with every course passed, as they hoped that failure would have presented solid reasons to suspend that particular course of study. As their true passions are being suppressed, they believe that they have no case to counter the position of their parents; after all, there is no beaten path to success and no lucrative job offer that awaits in the field they love. I do not believe that any parent would knowingly cause their child this type of pain. However, it does happen – and more often than you might believe. Hence, **it is vitally important to have open discussions with your child to find out what really matters to them and what makes them come alive.**

If you are a young person whose parents do not support your talents and interests, my best advice to you is to respect the views of your parents, while looking to your Heavenly Parent, God, for help and direction. **God knew you before your earthly parents did; He wrote the original script for your future and watches zealously that you walk in them.** Ephesians 2:10 is one of my favourite Bible verses. It says, "For we are His workmanship, created in Christ Jesus for good works, which God prepared beforehand that we should walk in them."[35] This passage gives me hope and comfort that I am not alone in my assignment on earth. I have heaven's help, and God is cheering me on.

If you are in this situation, first pray about your desires to confirm that they are indeed of God. After all, your parents could be correct in their views! If you are convinced that your interests are from God, then continue in peaceful confidence. You now know that you are on God's side, so it shall come to pass.

Second, **keep an open mind to the guidance of your parents, knowing that it is likely coming from a place of care**. In fact, the concerns of your parents will often provide useful information to caution you against rash decisions that can come from unbridled passion. Seek ways in which you can nurture your passions on the side, as you progress in what you are doing.

---

[34] Dreaded because the job offer was not in an area of their interest.
[35] NKJV.

Third, explore the various ways in which your talents could be expressed. Talk to people who are where you want to be, and see how you can forge a path from where you are now. Do not shy away from creating new paths – everything that is common today had a first time.

Finally, use this discomfort to build your character and develop the spiritual fruit of patience, perseverance, and faith in God. Recognize that nothing you do today will be wasted but that God is using every experience to weave the beautiful tapestry of your life. Indeed, He will cause all your knowledge and skills to come together for good as long as you keep yourself grounded in God.

The key point for parents to remember is that **the talents of your children are God-given gifts to guide them to fulfilling their purpose**. Talents are inherently valuable, so guide your children towards current, pertinent information to help them develop and employ their skills in ways for which they will be gainfully compensated. No matter the talent, applying the general success principles of hard work, passion, intuition, innovation and perseverance will create a path to career success. People will pay for anything that meets their needs in a feasible way.

Consider the talent of baking cookies. Imagine your child saying that they want to bake cookies when they are grown. Not many persons, maybe including you, would be impressed by this career choice. Perhaps a career in medicine, law, or aeronautics would seem more impressive. Introducing Debbi Fields, founder of Mrs. Fields Cookies, who is quoted as saying, "I knew I loved making cookies and every time I did, I made people happy."[36] Her husband said she wouldn't sell $50 worth of cookies the first day. After several hours in the shop with no sales, she assembled a tray of cookies and started to offer samples to the passers-by in the streets. By the end of the day, she rang up $75 in sales. Her husband would later become an integral part of the company's growth. The rest is history. The company grew into a multi-million dollar entity, with hundreds of outlets in several countries and employing thousands of people.

Just think that all Mrs. Fields could do was to bake cookies. But this was her talent and her passion. She recognized it and honoured this talent by developing it and creating a way for it to

---

[36] Let's Talk Business Network, Inc. 2007. The Network of Entrepreneur. Entrepreneur's Hall of Fame: Debbi Fields. http://www.ltbn.com/hall_of_fame/Fields.html (accessed November 09, 2016).

be of benefit to others. When she baked, she met needs and added value to the lives of people. Note also that in the process of honouring her talent of baking, she acquired other talents such as marketing, management, sales, communications, and many more. Every talent comes with the potential to be multiplied, and like a seed, when you plant it, you will reap many seeds. In the

(!) same way, **developing one talent will automatically attract the acquisition of other talents. Recognize your talents, embrace them, develop them, and release them to do good work**.

Are Personality Types Equal?

"The longer we live, the more we find we are like other persons."
– Oliver Wendell Holmes

(!) **Like talents, personality types are equal in essence and substance**. I am intrigued that God would hard-wire people so differently. At the core, we are the same, desiring good for ourselves and those we love; yet, from a baby exits the womb (or sometimes in the womb), one can note personality differences. Some babies are easy-going and have no issues with their wet diaper, while others pop out of the womb seemingly complaining about everything, including the temperature in the room.

I love to share a conversation that occurred between my sons when they were five and seven years old respectively. I was talking to them by phone from the hospital prior to them meeting their baby brother for the first time. I asked what they intended to say to the baby when they saw him. One child immediately blurted out, "Mom, I'm going to tell him that I love him!" The other child, in utter dismay at the pronouncement, exclaimed, "You can't say that; you don't even know him!" I smile each time I recall this exchange because the respective comments exactly capture their personalities. One child will jump and afterwards figure out the details of landing, while the other child must prove all things before accepting anything.[37]

(!) **For variety and balance, life does present us with people who have different personalities** – some are generally inclined to be doers, others talkers, some

---

[37] By the way, they are inseparable brothers.

supporters, while others are natural calculators. These are general personality predispositions that indicate the comfort zone of each person. For example, some people are very comfortable getting things done and find inaction to be an irritant, while others are more comfortable analyzing things and are disturbed by constant motion. **I believe that God deliberately hard-wires people with different personalities to set us up for inter-dependence, and to grant each person ample opportunity to develop character**. Through inter-dependence, we learn to appreciate the value that each personality brings to the table; and in choosing to leave our comfort zone to meet people on *their* terms, we develop patience, gentleness, and self-control.

Perhaps, like me, you have bemoaned your personality hard-wiring when you did not believe that your natural tendencies worked in your favour. Have you ever heard someone complain, "I wish I weren't so sensitive" or "I wish I weren't so direct"? Over the years, I have learned that my personality is not the issue; rather, it is my lack of self-knowledge and mastery that cause problems. Thus, **personality discontent is usually admittance of lack of self-mastery.** The enemy of your soul understands personality types too, and he continually entices you to ignore your need to develop self-control. A talkative personality can easily deteriorate into a gossip, while a calculating personality can easily deteriorate into a phobic. As a result, your personality is yours to control and master.

All personality types have the potential to bring value to a situation. However, in order for your personality to be of benefit, you will need to focus on the demands of the situation rather than on your personality. To do this, first determine the approach that will take you to the most favourable outcome, given the situation you are facing. Then, based on your knowledge of your personality, assess whether you are able to deliver what the situation requires or whether you will need help to so do. For example, if you are faced with a complaint, assess whether it requires you to listen or act. If you are a doer and the complaint requires action, you will have no problem responding from your comfort zone. However, if it requires that you listen and you are a talker, you will need to dig deep into your reservoir of self-control to respond accordingly. By removing your personality from the center of the issue – where it's no longer about you – to the periphery – where it becomes useful information to formulate a solution, you will automatically begin to think of how best to modify your personality tendencies to meet the needs of the situation.

We all have the ability to operate in various personality tendencies; however, depending on your hard-wiring, some tendencies will be much easier than others. The good news is that you will have ample practice, as you will be presented with situations on a daily basis that will require you to use all personality types to varying degrees. The key is being able to correctly assess the needs of each situation and respond accordingly. Given this reality, it is wise that you seek to strengthen those areas in your personality that require firmer management and ask for help when you know that the needs of a situation may be overwhelming.

Self-control is as much about what you make yourself do as it is about what you refrain from doing. For example, if resolution for a situation requires that you speak up and you know that you are uncomfortable asserting yourself, be willing ask someone who is assertive to help you to make your point.

Situation Response Checklist

Points	Notes
The key facts of the situation are (e.g., tensions from inaction):	
Personality attributes required for resolution (e.g., listening, patience, decision to act):	
Help needed to meet the demands for resolution (e.g., I am a cautious person, I will need support for decisiveness):	
I will get help from:	

(!) **It is advantageous to embrace and recognize the value that all personalities bring to the table**. So avoid the tendency to devalue your own personality and those of others. Instead, seek to learn from others and strive to increase your level of comfort by operating in all types of personality tendencies. For instance, my husband is a calculating supporter, while I am more of a talking doer. When we belittle the value that we each bring to the table, we make poor decisions and our marriage relationship deteriorates into disharmony. However, when we value the contribution of our respective personalities, we make better decisions, our marriage is harmonious, and we are more balanced as persons.

(!) **Guard against the tendency to recreate others in your own image.** This is one of the signals of an outlook that devalues personality types different from your own. I watched a documentary on Henry Ford, founder of the Ford Motor Company. He was mechanically gifted and had the dominant personality of a doer. He had one child, a son named Edsel. Unlike his father, Edsel was artistically gifted and had more of a supportive personality. Henry Ford would deliberately intimidate and humiliate his son, in what he later described as efforts to toughen him. Edsel appeared to have internalized stress, which resulted in stomach ulcer and cancer. He predeceased his father at the relatively young age of 49 years old.

My personal view on this story is that God blessed Henry Ford with a son whose talents and personality complemented his own. Henry Ford was gifted with mechanical genius and his son, Edsel, was gifted with design genius. What are the things people want most in a car? For it to perform well and look good. God equipped the Ford father-son duo with both. Unfortunately, Henry Ford fell into the trap that I and others often fall victim to – he wrongly thought he needed to duplicate himself in others (in this case, his son). Instead, it is better to seize the opportunities presented by complementarity. This approach affirms everyone's personality hardwiring and unites people in harmonious relationships for mutually beneficial outcomes. It is said that Henry Ford deeply regretted his actions towards his son whom he loved.

(!) **Seek to influence good character traits in others rather than trying to change their personalities. A**

good character will automatically inspire people to correct personality imbalances. For example, if you notice that someone with an introverted personality causes others to feel ignored, resist the temptation to compare them to others by saying, "Why can't you be like this or that extrovert?" Instead, raise their awareness of the impact of their actions and show them how investing time in others can enrich both their experiences and their relationships. If that person embraces thoughtfulness of character, they will feel compelled to sacrifice some of their "me time" to share in the things that bring joy to others. Each time they make this sacrifice, it will become easier the next time. **When people are influenced to build character, no one is pressured to mimic anyone but everyone is challenged to treat others with consideration, regardless of their personality hardwiring**.

Train Your Talents For Competence

Be diligent to present yourself approved to God, a worker who does not need to be ashamed, rightly dividing the word of truth.
– 2 Timothy 2:15 NKJV.

Competence is essential to meeting needs. Should I have an interest in dispensing medicine to treat the sick in my community, I would not be properly packaged if I simply decided to display a sign in my window that read *"Natalie Rowe – Medicine Woman."* That would neither work well for me nor for the sick. As a result, I must package my interest in medicine with the requisite knowledge and expertise that can be gained through study and practice. My certification in medicine would then be the signal to employers and to the market that I have prepared myself to effectively meet the needs of patients.

According to the Business Dictionary, competence is, "a cluster of related abilities, commitments, knowledge, and skills that enable a person to act effectively in a job or situation. Competence indicates sufficiency of knowledge and skills that enable someone to act in a wide variety of situations." Based on this definition, competence requires that a person is able, committed, knowledgeable, and skilled to effectively meet the need at hand.

Ability speaks to having the talent and capacity to act. If a task requires measurement, you should be able to do calculations. Commitment is dedicating yourself to the result. It is choosing to embrace an attitude of *stick-to-it-iveness* that leads to completion. Knowledge is having the requisite understanding and information about a subject that enables you to do a task. Skill speaks to knowing *how* to use the knowledge that you have to satisfy the demands of a situation.

Each of the four aspects of competence is necessary on their own, and neither one can replace the role of the other. They are much like the work of food nutrients in balanced nutrition, where each nutrient has a specific role. Carbohydrates, for example, cannot replace the role of proteins, nor can vitamins replace the role of fatty acids. So it is with competence. If you are able but not committed, the work will suffer just as much as if you are knowledgeable but not skilled. **Competence is developed through a combination of training and doing – both aspects are critical**. If your career requires writing, then continually improve your writing skills through practice and training. If it requires analytics, do the same. The only way to become better at a thing is to do more of that thing.

One of the most difficult actions that I've had to take in my capacity as a manager is to terminate an assignment due to incompetence for the required tasks. It weighed heavily on the person involved, on the team, and on me. It is uncomfortable and unfortunate, but I quickly learned that incompetence must be addressed, or very soon, it infects the entire team. No one appreciates having to clean up the muddle created by another person in addition to doing their own work; and to add insult to injury, take home the same pay! The experience taught me that it is better to absorb the pressure of inadequate personnel (while seeking to fill the deficit) than to rush into hiring someone who is not the right fit. I also learned that one of the best things I can do for my team is hire someone competent for the job in question. A competent person adds value to every team and will always be considered for a promotion or assignment. **Competence gets the job done and raises team productivity and morale.**

Train Your Personality for Positivity

"Your smile is your logo, your personality is your business card, how you leave others feeling after having an experience with you becomes your trademark." – Jay Danzie

It is said that 85% of workplace success is attributed to interpersonal skills.[38] This speaks to the importance of personality in career advancement. When I first came across this statistic, I was surprised at how much more people skills factored into career success than intelligence quotient. It is not always the brightest who go the furthest. More is achieved when intelligence goes hand-in-hand with people skills.

(!) **At the heart of a positive personality is the choice of one's focus.** The human brain can only focus on one mental activity at a time. For that reason, whatever holds your focus becomes bigger, as the act of focusing brings it to the foreground; simultaneously, other things become smaller as they fade into the background. You may have experienced allowing your mind to drift in the process of listening to someone speak. In no time, you are hearing nothing of what is said, even though the person may be standing in front of you.

According to Dr. Susan Weinschenk, behavioural psychologist, what we call multi-tasking is actually task-switching, which stresses the brain due to continual information retrieval from changing scenarios.[39] As a result, the act of multi-tasking actually makes us 40% less productive than if we were to focus on one task at a time.

You can use the knowledge of how focus works to your advantage. A good start is to eliminate the myth of "I had no choice" from your mind – you always have a choice.

(!) **Recognize that choices can be significantly limited but never eliminated**. You may not have had a choice as to where you were born, your parents, or your physical characteristics but you do have a choice on how you respond to your circumstances. In other words, even when you have no choice in the *what*, you still get to choose the *how*.

I am inspired by the story of a 92-year-old man who told his children that he wanted to be the first resident to move into a

---

[38] Study by Carnegie Foundation and Standard Research Institute at Harvard University.

[39] Weinschenk, Susan Ph.D. The True Cost Of Multi-Tasking – You Could Be Losing Up to 40% of Your Productivity. Psychology Today. https://www.psychologytoday.com/blog/brain-wise/201209/the-true-cost multi-tasking (accessed November 18, 2016).

retirement home that was under construction. When asked the reason for his curious pronouncement, he said that he wanted to be present to welcome and extend his friendship to the incoming residents whom he knows will likely be scared and lonely – wow! He could have complained about many things – not knowing anyone, why he had to go there, whether the food would be like his customary home-cooked meals, and on and on. Focus is indeed a choice. Needless to say, he made many friends, and has been a source of much comfort to the other residents. (Note also how this senior matched his talents with the needs of his environment – there is no expiry date on this principle!)

In your career, choose to focus on solutions rather than on obstacles. I outlined the benefits of this approach earlier in the book. Choosing to focus on solutions is not the same as ignoring the problem. It is rather seeking to understand the problem so well that you place yourself in a position to overcome it. Relocating to another city or even country represents major change, which can significantly impact your career. You may face setbacks, such as lack of recognition of your credentials, experiences, and professional level. You may also face language and other social barriers. However, there are things that you can do to increase your chances of success in the face of these obstacles.

Prior to relocating, **educate yourself on the requirements for operating in your career in your new city**. Expect that the more specialized your training, the greater the re-training that may be required to operate at a similar level in your new city. Research the required certifications and experiences, as well as the outlook and realities of newcomers. After assessing the career requirements, note where you fall short and identify activities and timelines to close each gap. If you require local work experience, explore volunteer opportunities; if language is a barrier, then enroll in language classes; if there is a cultural barrier, make friends and get involved in local activities.

My Canadian-born children influenced me to learn to ice-skate. I was hesitant at first since, being born in the tropics, I could more easily relate to fun in the sun than to fun on ice. Still, I went along with the idea, and in the process I embraced the humility of learning to keep off my bottom and on my feet. I also found that I enjoyed meeting new people. In fact, my first coach on the ice was a three year old who told me to "shimmy" if I ever wanted to start moving in the skates. In my embarrassment I smiled and asked her name. She replied, "Grace." *I thought, How fitting! I will be needing tons of grace* [40] *on this ice today.* It was all worth the spills and chills, and now I can engage with others in conversations around ice-skating (not that I am yet competent).

Continually remind yourself of the basic truth that careers spring from needs. So wherever you are, clue into the needs of your environment. Remain open and flexible. This assessment will help you to make an informed decision about relocating, shape realistic expectations about integrating in your new city, and overcome obstacles to your career.

Above all, purpose in your heart to embrace your new city. Care about where you live and work for the best of your new city. Do not permit yourself to be an extractor; that is, one who desires only to make money in one place so they can build a future elsewhere. Grow where you are planted, and love the people and the place in which you are growing. I invite you to do the following exercise to help you focus on solutions as you seek to function in your career.

Skills / Experiences Gap Checklist

Points	Notes
My career aspirations are:	
Required certifications/ experiences to operate in that career:	
Certifications/ experiences I possess:	
Certifications/ experiences I require:	
For each missing requirement/ experience, my plan (cost, time, means, etc.) to acquire them is:	

---

[40] In the sense of "divine help".

I am intrigued by the insights that flow when you apply your mind to the question of, "How could I make this work?" Compare that to the stress that is felt from, "Nothing will work." I reminisce with satisfaction on a decision I made in high school when I was faced with a challenging situation concerning one of my courses. It was a relatively new subject, and the school had difficulty sourcing and keeping teachers for this course. My colleagues, for the most part, were resigned to the unfavourable situation. However, I made a decision that I would pass the course. So, instead of waiting around for teachers to show up, I developed a plan of action to succeed. I went to the Ministry of Education and retained a copy of the course curriculum (we had no access to the Internet then), bought the recommended textbook, and began to take myself through it. By exam time, my classmates were only familiar with the parts of the curriculum that the teachers had taught. However, being familiar with the content of the entire curriculum, I passed the exam with ease. I recall the deputy headmistress inviting me to her office to congratulate me on the result – it was a first for the school in that course. Each time I recall this approach I took as a teenager, it reminds me of the importance of looking past obstacles and working solutions.

Whether you are starting your career, advancing in your career, or close to retirement, make choices that work to your advantage. If you choose to focus on the obstacle, it is a choice that you are making anyway; so why not make the choice work to your benefit? Obstacles can be sign posts pointing you to finding another way. I heard of an accountant who relocated to another country and started their own accounting practice when they could not land a job working for a firm. Obstacles can also be invitations to innovate, as in the accidental discovery of the chocolate chip cookie. Ruth Wakefield ran out of baker's chocolate and substituted a semi-sweet chocolate bar from Nestle in her cookie dough. The substitute ingredient softened instead of melting and the chocolate chip cookie was born.[41] So go ahead, give yourself permission to do something that you have never done before!

(!) As you intentionally focus on solutions, this habit will become engrained in your personality and manifest as positivity, motivation, leadership, and confidence. The very decision to continually solve challenges rather than be limited by them creates a virtuous cycle of engagement that excites and

[41] All about Chocolate Chip Cookies. http://iml.jou.ufl.edu/projects/fall09/saval_j/history.html (accessed November 20, 2016).

motivates you and the people around you. This will require you to take the lead in getting things done, and as this approach provides results, you will naturally grow in confidence. It is no secret that people who choose to be solutions-focused tend to get hired, promoted, and solicited for innovative projects.

Train Your Talents and Personality to Serve Your Career

Do not put the cart before the horse.

Now that you know the importance of training, before you step out, it is necessary to place the horse before the cart. Say this aloud a few times so that you can hear yourself – "**My studies must serve my career**." In other words, your career is the end, and your studies are a means to that end.

Too often, people default to studying and hoping for the best in getting hired. What would you think of someone who invested $25,000 (average cost of a Bachelor's degree) and said, "Ah well, I'm hoping for the best." I am certain that such an attitude would not inspire your confidence in handing over your money for them to invest on your behalf. However, many students do just this when it comes to their education. They continue into post-secondary studies without investing the effort to assess the realities of the job market and the prospect for a good return on their investment in post-secondary studies. This can be compounded by misaligned interests that result in switching majors that extend the time and cost of pursuing the program.

Education is more than studying for exams and obtaining certifications. It encompasses the whole slew of what you do to build expertise – volunteering, organizing, participating, and studying. **Accredited learning is still the most reliable signal to employers and potential clients of competence.** Studies have consistently shown that the higher the level of certification, the greater the earning potential. So achieving higher learning is worth the investment.

However, like a good investor, answer certain questions prior to investing your time, talents, and money in higher learning to ensure that you

are pursuing the right program for the right reasons. For emphasis, these include answers to self-awareness questions such as, "What are my natural talents and interests? What vocations am I likely to enjoy doing? Am I someone who likes to be on the frontline or in the background?" There are also the environment-awareness questions of what is happening within and among demographic groups; consumer preferences and trends. To answer these questions, research the skills demands of businesses and governments and educate yourself on social and economic indicators and trends.

If you feel overwhelmed about doing this yourself, there are organizations that offer services to help you answer these questions. The Internet, your community library, and your school are good places to start your research. **Educate yourself on vocational biases that may sway you from a fulfilling career**. For example, there tends to be a bias in favour of conventional degrees and away from technical training. You can minimize the chances of the undue influence of this bias by evaluating your answers to the preceding questions and choosing accordingly.

Assess the program offerings of post-secondary institutions to ensure that the content will equip you with the requisite skills to satisfy the demands of the job market. You may also research the opinion of employers on the workplace success of graduates coming from various types of post-secondary institutions. This will give you an idea of the skills that employers are seeking and the institutions that are preparing students accordingly. Instead of waiting for this information to come to you, seek it for yourself – the research effort will be well worth your time.

If you are still uncertain of a course of study to pursue, then the Gap Year is an option available to high school students to bridge them between secondary and tertiary studies. Parents are often doubtful of the idea of taking time off from institutionalized learning, as they fear their children may not return to school. However, studies show that 90% of students who took a Gap Year returned to college within a year. They also found that taking a Gap Year had a significant positive impact on students' academic performance in college. [42]A factor that influences this outcome is

---

[42] American Gap Association. National Alumni Survey 2015 Report. http://www.americangap.org/data-benefits.php (accessed March 15, 2016).

that the program is geared towards pursuing a career path through a structured approach that incorporates work experiences, career counselling, training in job search and interview skills, travelling and volunteering, and mentoring.

Gap Year programs are widespread in the United States and up and coming in Canada. [43]The Conference of Independent Schools in Ontario approves Gap Years and promotes the benefits that include increased maturity, focus, appreciation for university, and appeal to many universities.[44] They represent a win-win approach to helping students clarify their career path prior to investing thousands of dollars into certification with disappointing outcomes. Taking a structured Gap Year invariably serves to develop the individual into a more focused student with a better sense of purpose and engagement in the world.

I believe that it is also important to address the issue of amassing certifications in this section. I have witnessed cases where persons default to pursuing more certification and degrees in response to misaligned packaging. This may include resumes or cover letters that do not sufficiently capture skills and experiences. To avoid this limitation, **use the services of placement agencies or career counsellors to review your resumes**. At the very minimum, have someone else review it.

One job-seeker learned the value of getting a second eye on his resume the hard way. He was looking for work as a professional photographer of school and sports team pictures. Over a year and hundreds of resumes later, a recruiter contacted him because of an apparent error on his resume. Instead of stating, "Over 20 years in the photography industry," his resume read, "Over 20 years in the pornography industry." It appeared that his computer had incorrectly autocorrected the word photography. He was so grateful to have been alerted to this error. After making the correction on his resume, he landed a job a few weeks later.[45]

Another factor that can limit career advancement is weak interpersonal skills or an under-trained personality. It shows itself in one negative experience after another on the same job or with successive jobs, and the reason is always the fault of someone else. Yes, challenging people are everywhere, including in leadership. However, when you change situations

[43] MentorU Discover Year is a gap-year program in the cities of Ottawa and Toronto, Canada.
[44] Conference of Independent Schools of Ontario. http://www.cisontario.ca/page.cfm?p=294 (accessed March 15, 2016).
[45] Lair, Joanne. HR Horror Stories. HRPA Today. http://www.hrpatoday.ca/article/hr-horror-stories.html (accessed January 16, 2016).

and the challenge persists, this is usually a signal to take courage to introspect. **Self-examination is one of the habits of successful people, and given that the faults of others will always be there, progress requires you to examine your responses for areas of improvement.** After all, you are the only person over whom you have one hundred percent control, not others.

One person bitterly complained that their boss was the cause of their workplace challenges. Sometime later, when asked about their situation in light of a new boss, they commented that nothing had changed because the previous boss had poisoned the mind of the current boss prior to leaving the position (pause and think about that). Even so, the person clearly assumed that the new boss was incapable of assessing the veracity of the report from the previous boss. Self-examination takes courage. **No one enjoys having to admit to their failures, but the price of avoidance is self-imposed imprisonment.** Too many smart and talented people are frustrated and limited because they fail to realize that their limitation is on the inside, and it can only be removed by self-examination and change.

Another possible sign of a personality limitation is finding yourself alone in promoting your competence. That is, no one else *voluntarily* [46] endorses your candidature to others. It is so much easier when your competence and positive attitude talk on your behalf because they are loaded with credibility. Others can easily run with this reputation and promote your candidature to others. It is a very humbling experience when this happens, and the only "pressure" is the desire to continue doing your best. Let me quickly add that this advice does not eliminate the importance of communicating your career aspirations to others. However, your competence and personality will amplify your verbal message and do the heavy-lifting on your behalf.

It follows that a wrong diagnosis of a limiting factor will lead to a wrong prescription. As such, **seek to accurately identify the reason for any struggles you may be experiencing in your career, rather than to default to additional certification**. It is very painful to observe unnecessary investment to acquire more certification, as it comes at a high cost in time and money and results in even greater expectations

---

[46] Without you having to ask.

for promotion. I find that this response is a "set up" for greater disappointment and bitterness towards everyone and everything.

It takes courage to acknowledge limiting factors that are personal. It will also take great effort to address them. Someone shared with me that **success is directly linked to the number of difficult conversations a person is willing to entertain**. Identifying any personal limitation to your career will likely involve a difficult conversation that will include honest self-assessment. Again, that choice is yours.

Power Perspectives for Trained Talents and Personality

What if you were to embrace the perspective that, *"It is my responsibility to ensure that my studies prepare me for my work."* A purposeful life requires that one start at the end (by envisioning your goals), work backwards through planning, then move forward by working your plans. Specifically, write down where you see yourself in two years, five years, ten years, and at the end of your life. Begin to work backwards from your vision to where you are today. Then, identify the things that you must do to take you to that desired end. Now for the fun part – start doing them!

Career Path Plan

What will I do in retirement?	
Where do I see myself in twenty years?	
Where do I see myself in ten years?	
Where do I see myself in two years	
Things I will do to reach my goals in two years	
How do my career goals support each other?	

This approach to pursuing your dreams ensures alignment. I have always felt that the most difficult decisions in life are often choices among attractive options – which good thing do I apply myself to? The appropriate response should be informed by your vision and purpose for life. I have endured a few presentations on business proposals in which I declined to invest. Sometimes, the presenters were not convinced that I believed the proposal to be profitable. I explained that I did in fact see the profitability of the proposal but it did not align with my vision for my life. Realizing the profits, for example, might require me to dedicate significant amounts of time away from my family, which is not something that I am willing to do. In other cases, the nature of the business did not in any way interest me, so I knew that I would bring no passion to the process.

These are the benefits of having a general sense of the direction for your life. It helps you to focus your efforts because your time and other resources at your disposal are finite, and not every need is your call. If you are in a place of uncertainty concerning your future, do not panic. Review and act on the S.E.T. steps discussed in this book, and over time, you should find that you will begin to narrow your options.

Another benefit of alignment is that it positions you for maximum performance. When we change the tires on our vehicles, my husband habitually takes the car to the dealership for alignment. I questioned the value of this expenditure, given that the tires were new. I learned that wheel alignment increases fuel efficiency, protects against uneven and premature wear on the vehicle, extends the life of the tires, and provides for a smoother driving experience. With this understanding, I now see the expenditure as an investment.

Similarly, **when you align your education to meet the demands of your work, you will minimize the amount of time you spend studying, experience a smoother transition into the workforce or into business**, be more efficient in what you do, and enjoy the benefits of career satisfaction, security, and success.

I recommend that you go through the S.E.T. steps as often as required, especially when you are at the crossroads of a career decision or when you require affirmation for a decision made.

Summarizing Trained Talents and Personality

I concur with the idea that icing makes people eat cake. The more beautiful the decoration on a cake, the more I want to sink my teeth into it. I have bought products and services of inferior quality because I was misled by the attractive packaging. I am also certain that I have passed over quality products and services because of unattractive packaging. The ideal state is to have quality products and services that are attractively packaged.

Likewise, **your talents and personality are intrinsically valuable, so make every effort to package them well**. Train your talents to develop competence for your work, and train your personality to embrace a positive mindset to serve others.

I heard the story about an ex-convict who had completed his prison term for financial fraud committed when he was the CFO of a large corporation. He was asked about his time in prison among hardened criminals. He responded that it was not difficult, as he made friends by making himself useful. He explained that, being highly literate among semi-literate and illiterate inmates, he used his skills to read and interpret documents, and write letters on their behalf. This example confirms that when the combination of competence and positive attitude are used to meet the needs around you, they work – even in prison! This also reminds me of Proverbs 18:16a that says, "A man's gift makes room for him."[47] Indeed, the technical and interpersonal skills of this convict made room for him in prison. He earned protection and a sense of usefulness during an unfortunate period of his life.

Choose to value every talent that you uncover and accord them the respect of nurture and development. I was talking to a realtor who recommitted to dedicating time from his busy schedule to nurture his passion for screen-writing. Real estate and screen-writing do not seem like natural matches, but who knows how these two interests could coalesce, and the blessings that could flow from them? I applauded his decision to nurture all his passions.

The devaluing of a talent starts with the thought process. The moment you entertain thoughts such as, "I have no talent, I can never do anything right, or what I can

---

do is of little value," these thoughts serve to marginalize what you have and hinder any opportunity for development. As you meditate on those deceptions, you will begin to make decisions that will stifle your talents and, in effect, your career. The same is true for your personality type. Do not regret your hard-wiring, as it was given to you for productive purposes. Invest the time to understand your hard-wiring and those of others. Develop your self-control muscle through the practice of leaving the comfort zone of your personality type and operating in the personality tendencies for which you are uncomfortable. Place the needs of the situation that you are facing at the center (instead of your personality), and identify the responses that will best get to a resolution. Then adjust your response accordingly, or get help to do so.

(!) **The pursuit of competence will make a way for you and automatically lead you to acquiring and uncovering more talents**. Choosing a positive attitude will keep you operating on the frontier of breakthroughs and insights, and position you to create ever-increasing value for yourself and others. Ensure that your investment in learning and acquiring certification is continually serving your career. In other words, before you commit time and resources into higher learning, ensure that the acquired knowledge will satisfy the skill needs of your intended career. This will require you to be proactive in seeking information on current and trending skills demands. Place the onus on yourself to ensure that your investment in learning positions you to reap the dividends that you seek. Do not delegate the responsibility of packaging yourself for career success.

Conclusion

The three aspects to examine prior to proceeding in your career – self-awareness, environment-awareness, trained talents and personality – represent a winning mindset for proceeding and succeeding in your career. It starts with knowing that you are born for a purpose that your personality, interests, and talents have equipped you to realize. It also involves knowing that needs are ever present to be met, and that your career is about identifying the needs that align with your hard-wiring.

The pursuit of your career may seem like a fishing expedition that takes you out into a vast ocean that is full of possibilities. For a successful catch, cast your line into the sections of the water where your hard-wiring (personality, interests, talents) intersects with the needs around you. This approach answers the question of "where to fish" for your career. Then take advantage of the opportunities around you to focus your career choice.

In positioning for your chosen career, prepare your talents to respond to needs in a way that adequately compensates you. This means preparing your talents so they will be in demand by the labour market. Ensure that your fishing line is reinforced with competence and baited with a positive attitude. This combination will guarantee that opportunities will continuously bite at your bait. Fishing for your career in the right place, with the right approach, and with the right competences will position you to enjoy the satisfaction of lifelong work.

As I continue my own career journey, I face the uncertainties and excitement of the future. However, I am anchored and propelled by self-knowledge and information on the needs of my environment. Like a GPS, I am using this information to guide my exploration of ways to meet needs that coincide with my hard-wiring, add value to others, and compensate my efforts. Furthermore, the knowledge that I have found that which makes me come alive injects confidence in my career decisions and cheers each step forward.

Epilogue

Career exploration and success is a very personal experience. Rather than being linear; it can be like a jungle gym that provides several options to move you upward because you are a dynamic being who is continuously evolving to impact a dynamic world. Your talents and personality are alive with the potential for increase and can be reinvented, retrained, and repackaged to meet the needs of your environment in ever-changing ways.

There is no limit to the frequency or to the stage in life to which these S.E.T. principles can be applied. As long as you have a pulse, always consider how you can better meet the needs of your world. This journey can be even more exciting in retirement when people tend to feel more liberated to do the things they have always desired but may have been too risk-averse to pursue.

With these can-do perspectives, you can indeed enjoy a life of satisfaction, meaning and career success.

Now that you are S.E.T., go!

Appendix: 1

S.E.T Checklist for Career Success

Career aspect	Indices	My action plan to progress
The value in obstacles	When I see obstacles, I: * Am energized to overcome them because... * Discouraged and annoyed because... * Neutral because...	I will: * Identify the value in the obstacle. * Decide if I want that value and will pay the price. * Research the most effective way of overcoming the obstacle.
The process of worth transfer	* I look forward to working hard because ... * I don't like pressuring myself because...	I will: * List all the benefits of the pursuit (physical, emotional, $$). * List all the cost of the pursuit (physical, emotional, $$). * Make a clear choice and see it through to the end.

Career aspect	Indices	My action plan to progress
Trying uncovers help	Normally I: * Step out before I have a clear plan because… * Need the complete picture before I proceed because…	I will: * Make a workable plan before stepping out. * Identify help needed and where to get it.
Paradox of the comfort zone	* I do not enjoy challenges because… * I like new and unpredictable situations because…	I will: * Determine if I wish to grow or stay the same. * Have a general approach to respond to unplanned situations.

Career aspect	Indices	My action plan to progress
Nudge Forward	* The things I do in excess are... * The things that others tell me I do in excess are... * The opportunity cost of these excesses are... * I believe that I am where I should be because ... * I believe that I need to move on because...	I will: * List the things that I want to accomplish in life. * Make a SMART plan to realize them. * Allocate my time to meet my plans. * Create my exit strategy when I know it's time to move on. * Identify my signals to move on and list possibilities for next steps.
What I care about and do well	I know my (TIP): * Talents: ... * Interests: ... * Personality style: ...	I will: * Seek more information on... * Get more involved in... to discover more about my ...

Career aspect	Indices	My action plan to progress
What others say I do well	* The things that others say about my personality are... * The things that others say I do well are...	I will: * Compare the feedback of others with my own views. * Seek professional/ third-party assessment to confirm and improve.
Confidence in my talents (My talents are always in demand to meet needs. It is skills that need to be updated).	My skills: * Are in (high, steady, low) demand * Will adequately compensate me	I will: * Package/ repackage my skills to meet demands by ... * Explore ways to create demand for my skills by ...

Career aspect	Indices	My action plan to progress
Job security	When I think of losing a job/ having lost a job, I: * Felt like my expertise were tied to that job * Found it difficult/ easy to detach myself from that job * Felt pessimism/ optimism about my prospects for a new job	To take control of my income security, I will: * Keep abreast of changing consumer demands and their impact on my skills. * Update my skills accordingly. * Act in the awareness that my expertise are inalienable. * Remember that jobs go into recession, not needs.
The needs around me	* The needs of others that appeal to my interests … * The systems and processes that animate/ annoy/ attract me…	I will: * Research existing and emerging jobs and careers. * Find out the requirements to starting my own business. * Imagine new ways of using my talents to meet needs.

Career aspect	Indices	My action plan to progress
Connecting my talents to needs	I could work as a: * Name the area… * Identify the job… * Name the business…	I will: * Talk to someone who is where I want to be. * Job-shadow in an area of my interest. * Research the skills demand of private, public, and NGO sectors.
Guaranteeing my work	I can easily see myself as a: * Professional * Entrepreneur * My reasons are … * I agree/disagree that workers are also entrepreneurs. My reasons are…	I will: * Listen to others and ask clarifying questions to better understand their needs – e.g., what would make this better for you? * Consider and act in ways that improve the service I offer to others. * Make this attitude a way of life at home, school and work.

Career aspect	Indices	My action plan to progress
My competencies	I am: * Able to do... * Knowledgeable in... * Skilled in... * Persistent (I see things through to the end)	I will: * Seek ways to practice... * Get more knowledge in... * Develop skills in... by ... * Strengthen my commitment by ...
Positive attitude	* I see the glass as: * Half-full because... * Half-empty because... * Halfway because... * I see myself as an optimist, pessimist, realist. * Others see me as an optimist, pessimist, realist. * I am comfortable/ not/ neutral re my worldview because...	I will: * Practice to assess all aspects of a situation – positive and negative by ... * Practice to focus on solutions by ...

Career aspect	Indices	My action plan to progress
Certify to serve my career	* I solicit professional advice prior to signing up for a program. * I pursue courses as a default. * Others confirm that I am open to constructive feedback.	* Before pursuing the next course, I will: * Review the S.E.T. Checklist. * Identify a valid reason for pursuing the course. * Consult an independent professional third-party to confirm course necessity. * Submit myself to a personal assessment review.